THOMAS MERTON
My Brother

THOMAS MERTON
My Brother

His Journey to Freedom, Compassion,
and Final Integration

essays by
M. Basil Pennington

New City Press

Published in the United States by New City Press
202 Cardinal Rd., Hyde Park, NY 12538
©1996 Cistercian Abbey of Spencer, Inc.

Cover: Oil portrait of Thomas Merton by Randall S. Browning (1993)
©1993 Randall S. Browning. Used with permission.

Photo on page ii: "Official Portrait of Thomas Merton"
by John Howard Griffin (1963)
©1990 Elizabeth Griffin-Bonazzi. Used with permission.

Library of Congress Cataloging-in-Publication Data:

Pennington, M. Basil.
    Thomas Merton, my brother : his journey into freedom, compassion,
and final integration / M. Basil Pennington.

    Includes bibliographical references.
    1. Merton, Thomas, 1915-1968.   2. Trappists--United States--
Biography.   3. Spirituality--Catholic Church--History--20th
century.   4. Catholic Church--Doctrines--History--20th century.
I. Title.
BX4705.M542P47   1996
271'.12502--dc20
[B] 255.125   95-34530

Printed in the United States of America

Contents

Welcome

I remember the day well. It was December 10, 1968. I had just finished going through my mail. There was a picture postcard from Tom—a rather garish picture from Singapore. The message was brief enough and rather business-like:

> Dear Basil:
> It has been the custom for the Abbot to sign all my contracts so I am returning the one for *Climate* to Brother Patrick; he will see it is properly executed. I guess I ought to read the galleys, but I am not sure where I will be.

And then very significantly:

> Asia has been magnificent so far and more to come.

I clipped the stamp from the card for my brother who collects stamps and dropped the card into the wastebasket. Then I went up to the cloisters.

Father Abbot was tacking a note to the bulletin board. I stood beside him and read it in silence:

> Word has just been received that Thomas Merton died today in Bangkok.

We said nothing but went down the stairs and out into the bracing air of a December day. We walked side by side in silence, appreciating the comforting presence of each other, each with our own thoughts.

7

It had been a year of repeated shocks: The martyrdom of Martin Luther King. Thanks to him we all had a dream. The blighting of America's hope in the insane slaying of Robert Kennedy, our friend, who now lies under the simple white cross of the Cistercians in Arlington cemetery near his more famous brother. And now Tom—Thomas Merton, our own dear Father Louis, my brother monk with whom I had shared so much.

I remembered well our first meeting. I had just arrived at Gethsemani for a regional meeting of the Cistercian abbots. A terrible cold had gotten hold of me and I had a high fever. I quickly found my room in the guest house and buried myself in the warm blankets. I wanted nothing but the sweet and healing oblivion of sleep.

But I was no sooner settled in than a knock came at the door. It was my impetuous brother Tom who came sailing in under full steam. The eremitical life was still a long-sought-for goal in his life. And he was pursuing it with eagerness. I was at that time involved with the Second Vatican Council as a so-called *periti* (expert) as well as one of the canonists of the Cistercian Order. A new Code of Canon Law was in the offering and new constitutions for the Order. Merton wanted to make sure that both of these pieces of legislation, and the Council too, made provision for the eremitical life. He had in hand a paper which he thrust upon me, even though my head was too clouded with fever to read it. It was an *apologia* for the eremitical life. It was marked "strictly confidential." But I noted that it was in fact mimeographed, which meant that there were probably a hundred "strictly confidential" copies floating around. So typical of Tom. We enjoyed—after my fever abated—a very rich week together.

Our work together would continue and take many forms. Both of us were blessed with a good classical education. And both of us found, when we entered the Cistercian novitiate, that most of the very inspiring writings of our Cistercian

Fathers were available only in their original Latin, and most of our fellow novices could not comfortably read this language. So we both began translating texts of Saint Bernard and other Fathers for our brothers. In fact, Tom's first published work was a small book entitled *The Spirit of Simplicity: Characteristic of the Cistercian Order,* in which he translated not only a report of the Order's General Chapter but also a very fine selection of texts from Saint Bernard's sermons on the Song of Songs. Sensitive to our brothers' needs and conscious of the Second Vatican Council's call to renewal by means of returning to the spirit of our founders, Tom and I collaborated in 1968, the last year of his life, in the founding of Cistercian Publications. It had the precise purpose of making all the writings of our Cistercian Fathers available in the English language, as well as studies about them and other aspects of the monastic life. Tom's final postcard, quoted above, referred to the first volume we were to publish, his own *Climate of Monastic Prayer.*

One rarely writes a formal biography of one's brother. Rather, memories are shared, vignettes are drawn. And that is precisely what I offer here. Over the years, at the request of one publisher or another, one conference organizer or another, I have written papers sharing my memories of Tom, my sense of him drawn from our meetings, correspondence and his many published and unpublished writings. Some of the papers are more formal and scholarly in form, responding to the occasion proposed; others are more informal and personal. Each seeks to illumine some particular facet of this multifaceted monk.

One of Tom's favorites among the Fathers was a fifth-century Syrian monk, who adopted the name of Dionysius the Areopagite, usually referred to as the Pseudo-Dionysius. Dionysus taught us that there are three kinds of contemplation: *Direct,* like centering prayer or prayer of the heart, whereby we plunge directly into the divine. We will speak more about this further on, for it was in the end Tom's way of prayer. *Oblique*, when we find the divine through "the works of his hand," through his creation. In my paper below on the Byzantine influence in Tom's life, I will indicate what a profound role this played in his spiritual development. And *circular*, when one circles around the object of contemplation, gathering in, one after the other, different aspects, gradually enriching one's sense of the whole. This collection of papers, many of which have been published before, though some in journals and books not easily come upon, are so many moments in circular contemplation of a truly great human person, one who had the courage to come to final integration through living to the full his chosen vocation of a monk. Don't be surprised at some repetitions. Some facets do stand out and ask to be looked at more than once. Each of us can only be enriched by increased contact with Thomas Merton, Father Louis, even if it be only through his writings.

Following the introduction, I am offering a chronology of Merton's all too brief life. This may help to put these different vignettes into the context of the whole. But it will be of more value to you the reader if you can let each one of them add something to your own inner image of this wonderful, intensely human man, who really got hold of what it means to be a Christian and a monk, and who joyfully and fearlessly sought to live it to the full without rejecting in any way the fullness of his humanity.

Enjoy Thomas, my brother, as you read these pages. For it is with joy that I share them with you, wishing I could share so much more of him with you.

Father M. Basil, O.C.S.O.

Introduction

When an idealistic young man, Thomas Merton or any other, enters a monastery he "leaves the world behind." And all too soon he discovers that in the gate with him has snuck the biggest problem he had had "out in the world"—himself, with a memory well stored and ready to play reruns. The first paper in this collection, and indeed in one way or another all the papers in this collection, look at how Merton dealt with this problem and its many ramifications as he pursued his ideal.

Merton was a man of extraordinary genius with a background that enabled him to develop that genius in many extraordinary ways. When he set his heart on becoming a Cistercian he applied his genius to that task. As the Second Vatican Council would later advise, one of the steps on the way to becoming a good Cistercian is to get in touch with the spirit and aims of the founders of the Order. In a way that would be impossible for most aspirants, Merton spent many long hours during his first years in the monastery with the Cistercian Fathers in their writings. At that time these Fathers were available for the most part only in the intimidating volumes compiled by P.J. Migne: small print, large tomes, all in Latin.

Young Frater Louis, as Merton was then called, came to love these Fathers and their Latin. He tried hard in later years to get his choir novices, who supposedly had the necessary Latin background, to delve into the richness that lay hidden in the Fathers' writings. He was remarkably successful in some cases. Yet, he did admit the need to make the Fathers' thought available in translation if more than a chosen few were to be exposed to it. He did a certain amount of translating himself in those early days, and later encouraged others to do the same.

It was out of a shared vision, responding to an admitted need, that we obtained the sponsorship of the American abbots to begin Cistercian Publications in 1968. Father Louis' first contribution, his own manuscript *The Climate of Monastic Prayer*, was an expansion of an essay he had written some years earlier. It included some material from an earlier unpublished manuscript, and in its later sections some very deep sharing of Merton's own prayer experience, cast in the impersonal mode in accord with his usual reticence in regard to his own prayer life.

Before that volume, our first, was published, Father Louis completed his journey. The publications project went on, receiving continuing inspiration and, I am sure, heavenly benediction from our departed brother.

There is a remarkable complementarity among the papers in this book, which meld together to present a well-rounded presentation of Merton's multifaceted journey toward the realization of his ever cherished ideal. I will not endeavor to summarize them here, or even offer a synthesis, but perhaps I can offer a single guiding thought.

Father Louis was an existentialist in the best sense of the word. For him, what was important was what is—not thoughts or ideas, but reality experienced. He came into a real experience of God, of his relation with God, and of the absolute centrality of this relationship. In that experience he resolved to let go of all to be to God. Yet, some consciousness of his oneness with all others—this gospel truth is too clearly stated to be ignored—confronted him. He struggled with this until the breakthrough on the corner of Fourth and Walnut.[1] (One of the many things that must keep Tom laughing in heaven is

---

1. See chapter below, "Growing into Compassion," p. 29.

the sight of fervent Merton pilgrims wandering down Fourth in search of the famous corner—and their eventual shock when they discover it is now Fourth and Ali Mohammed! How he must love that!) With this Louisville experience came the freedom and the necessity to be to all. Then came more struggle—now because of the institution within which he lived and the formation it sought to give, one that did not necessarily flow from a deeper contemplative insight, from a powerful grasp of reality.

I think it is necessary to see all that Thomas Merton wrote before and after this experience in the light of the absence or presence of it. Obviously, it is not a question of an absolute black and white. What broke forth in a hymn of thanksgiving that day was always there within and, in subtle and not so subtle ways, had its impact on the man, monk and writer. Before that day he knew by faith and concept the reality of his solidarity—as do most of us. After that experience he had to struggle continually against the weight of the prevailing previous formation in the Cistercian Trappists. But a very profound shift in consciousness had taken place, and it radically affected the course of his development and orientation.

The reality of his solidarity with every man, woman and child on this planet meant that he could in no way attempt to be to God without his fellow humans. As long as any one of them was held back by un-freedoms that chained—such as those most blatantly present in racial prejudice expressed in segregation warfare—he had to anguish over them and, in accord with his vocation as a monk and writer, had to pray and speak out for the conversion which would bring freedom.

Merton came to know, in the way that only profound enlightened experience can teach, that he could never again seek to close out anyone in the world and seek to be to God without them. We are all in this together. There is but one humanity to the Father in Christ. There is no other way to be truly to God. There is no other way to be. Every attempt at being without God and without every other human person is illusion.

The journey to full human integration is what life is all about for Thomas Merton, for any monk or nun, for any Christian, for any human being. We have in Thomas Merton, monk, Christian, man, a marvelously inspiring guide and a companion for the journey, just because he was so truly human, so deeply Christian, and so much a monk—a man for every man and woman.

A Merton Chronology

1915   January 31, born in Prades, France.
1916   Moves to the United States with his parents.
1921   October 3, his mother, Ruth Jenkins Merton, dies of cancer.
1922   October 22, goes to Bermuda with his father.
1923   Returns to Douglaston, New York, to live with Ruth Merton's parents.
1925   Moves to France with his father; they settle at St. Antonin.
1926   Begins studies at Lycée Ingres, Montauban, France.
1927   Summer, lives with the Privats in Murat, France.
1928   May, moves to England and continues his studies at Ripley Court.
1929   Easter, at Canterbury with his father.
       August, goes to Aberdeen, Scotland, and his father enters the hospital in London.
       Fall, enters Oakham Public School in Rutland, England.
1930   June, Grandfather Jenkins gives him financial independence.
       Christmas recess, goes to Strasbourg.
1931   January 18, his father, Owen Merton, dies of a brain tumor.
       Easter recess, goes to Florence and Rome.
       Summer, visits the United States.
       Fall, editor of the *Oakhamian;* writes on Gandhi.
1932   Easter recess, visits Germany.
       September, attains a higher certificate.
       December, wins a scholarship to Clare College, Cambridge.
1933   February, goes across France to Rome for a prolonged visit.
       Summer, visits the United States.
       Fall, begins classes at Cambridge.
1934   Summer, visits the United States.
       Fall, returns to England to obtain resident visa for the United States.
1935   January, begins classes at Columbia University.
       Spring, joins and leaves the Communist party.

1936   October 30, his grandfather, Samuel Jenkins, dies.

1937   Editor of the Columbia *Yearbook;* art editor of the *Jester.*
        February, reads Etienne Gilson's *The Spirit of Medieval Philoso-*
        phy.
        August 16, his grandmother, Martha Jenkins, dies.

1938   Receives his Bachelor of Arts degree and begins to work for
        his Master of Arts.
        August, Mass at Corpus Christi.
        Fall, moves to 114th Street apartment; studies under Daniel
        Walsh.
        November 16, baptized as a Roman Catholic.

1939   February 22, receives his Master of Arts degree.
        Visits Bermuda; moves to Perry Street in the Village.
        Teaches at the Columbia University Extension and writes
        book reviews for the New York newspapers.
        May 29, receives the sacrament of Confirmation.
        Summer, lives at Olean, New York, with Lax and Rice; writes
        The Labyrinth.
        Fall, begins teaching English at Saint Bonaventure's College.
        November, applies to join the Franciscans.

1940   April-May, visits Cuba.
        June, rejected as an applicant to the Franciscan order.
        Summer, at Olean.

1941   Easter, retreat at the Abbey of Gethsemani, Trappist, Ken-
        tucky.
        September, retreat at Our Lady of the Valley Monastery,
        Cumberland, Rhode Island.
        December 10, enters the Abbey of Gethsemani.

1942   February 21, receives the novice's habit and his monastic
        name of Frater Louis.

1944   March 19, temporary profession.
        Thirty Poems.

1946   *A Man in the Divided Sea.*

1947   March 19, solemn profession, consecration as a monk.

1948   August 4, death of Dom Frederic Dunne.
        August 23, election of Dom James Fox.
        December 21, ordained subdeacon.
        Exile Ends in Glory; Figures for an Apocalypse; The Seven Storey
        Mountain; The Spirit of Simplicity; What Is Contemplation?

1949 May 26, priestly ordination.
The Tears of the Blind Lions; Seeds of Contemplation; The Waters of Siloe.

1950 *Selected Poems; What Are These Wounds?*

1951 May, master of students.
The Ascent to Truth.

1952 July, visit to Ohio.
Bread in the Wilderness; The Sign of Jonas.

1954 *The Last of the Fathers.*

1955 Master of novices.
No Man Is an Island.

1956 *The Living Bread; Praying the Psalms; Silence in Heaven.*

1957 *The Basic Principles of Monastic Spirituality; The Silent Life; The Strange Islands; The Tower of Babel.*

1958 March 18, the enlightenment at Fourth and Walnut.
Monastic Peace; Nativity Kerygma; Thoughts in Solitude.

1959 *The Secular Journal of Thomas Merton; Selected Poems of Thomas Merton.*

1960 October, building of the hermitage on Mount Olivet.
Disputed Questions; Spiritual Direction and Meditation; The Wisdom of the Desert.

1961 *The Behavior of Titans; The New Man; New Seeds of Contemplation.*

1962 *Clement of Alexandria; Original Child Bomb; A Thomas Merton Reader.*

1963 Awarded medal for excellence by Columbia University.
Breakthrough to Peace; Emblems of a Season of Fury; Life and Holiness.

1964 Honorary Doctorate of Letters, University of Kentucky.
Come to the Mountain; Seeds of Destruction.

1965 August 20, formally enters the hermitage.
Gandhi on Non-Violence; Seasons of Celebration; The Way of Chuang Tzu.

1966 *Conjectures of a Guilty Bystander; Hagia Sophia; Raids on the Unspeakable.*

1967 *Mystics and Zen Masters.*

1968 January 13, election of Father Flavian Burns as abbot of Gethsemani.
May, visits California and Arizona.

September, visits around the country and then Asia.
December 10, dies in Bangkok, Thailand.
Cables to the Ace; Faith and Violence; Zen and the Birds of Appetite.

1969 *Climate of Monastic Prayer* (later published as *Contemplative Prayer); The Geography of Lograire, My Argument with the Gestapo; The True Solitude.*

1970 *Opening the Bible.*

1971 *Contemplation in a World of Action; Early Poems: 1940-1941; Thomas Merton on Peace.*

1972 *The Asian Journal of Thomas Merton; Cistercian Life.*

1975 *He Is Risen.*

1976 *Ishi Means Man.*

1977 *The Collected Poems of Thomas Merton; A Hidden Wholeness* (with John Howard Griffin), *The Monastic Journey.*

1978 *A Catch of Anti-Letters* (with Robert Lax).

1979 *Letters from Tom; Love and Living.*

1980 *Thomas Merton on Saint Bernard.*

1981 *Day of a Stranger; Introductions East and West; The Literary Essays of Thomas Merton.*

1983 *Woods, Shore, Desert.*

1985 *The Hidden Ground of Love; Letters.*

1986 *The Alaskan Journal of Thomas Merton.*

1989 *The Road to Joy; Letters.*

1990 *The School of Charity; Letters.*

1992 *The Springs of Contemplation.*

1994 *The Courage of Truth; Letters;*
Witness to Freedom; Letters.

1995 *Run to the Mountains; Journals.*

The Seven Freedoms:
Thomas Merton's Quest for True Freedom

Thomas Merton's life falls into two equal parts. Merton entered the Cistercian Trappist monastery of Gethsemani, on December 10, 1941, just before his twenty-seventh birthday. He died on December 10, 1968, felled by electric shock and heart attack at a monastic meeting in Bangkok. For the first six years of each of these periods there stood over him a parental figure who encouraged him in the use and development of his most outstanding gift, that of being a writer. In the one case, it was his mother, Ruth Merton, who died when her son was six; in the other, it was his first abbot, Dom Frederic Dunne, who died six years after Merton entered Gethsemani.

For the rest, though, the climb up the seven mountains of Dante's *Purgatorio* "to win his freedom" was an uneven struggle.

Free by Nature

Ruth Merton, with her husband seconding her efforts, was determined to make of her son Tom a man who would stand on his own two feet. When later he did take his strong, stubborn stands against her authority, she may have been tempted to regret her training. But Tom did grow into a man who could stand on his own and do what he really wanted to do.

Freedom has the inherent quality of being able to be abused as well as used. Orphaned before he was sixteen, Tom did abuse his freedom. And he learned by his mistakes. Later he saw how "for those who love God all things work together unto good"—even sin. His native, well-developed freedom was there as a solid basis for the activity of grace, which must always build on nature. If parents, educators, or even a church deliberately or unconsciously inhibit the growth of persons' freedom, they not only truncate those persons' full development as human beings but block the growth of the Christ-life within them. In one of his last articles published before his death, Merton decried the danger that institutional religion, even monasteries, might foster human freedom only up to a point and then seek to place a cap on it, so that the "subject" might remain subject.

Freedom of Faith

Merton learned painfully that undisciplined freedom soon enough leads to the loss of freedom, at least the freedom to do what one really wants to do with one's life. His license at college not only lost him his scholarship and career but also his relationship with his guardian. He was not able to leave all this behind him as easily as he left England behind. But his life did start to take a new direction in the new world.

Merton realized the need to ground his new life on some solid principles—solid enough to satisfy a deeply questioning and perceptive mind. When he was finally able to free himself from inbred prejudices, he found the principles he sought in the Catholic faith. On this solid rock of truth he was able to find the firm footing he needed to exercise his freedom to the full. But it would be a while yet before he would be able to do that. He still needed something more: discipline.

Freedom of Monasticism

It is one thing to know the truth, another to be able to live by it. Years of license leave their mark. A wild and unruly freedom needs strong restraints to be brought into harness so that its power can be fully directed.

Merton needed discipline. Lay Catholic life did not seem to provide it in sufficient strength for him. He looked to religious life and finally found what he was seeking in what was then considered the strictest order in the Church: the Cistercians of the Stricter Observance, commonly called Trappists. When its rules began to fully regulate Merton's life, his poetic spirit blossomed, and he produced some of his best poetry and most profound prose.

Free to Be to the World

But monasticism itself, with its high ideal, caught this idealistic writer in its web. Merton got caught, as he himself confessed, in a "dream of separateness, of spurious self-isolation in a special world, the world of renunciation and supposed holiness." And it was a dream, a truly Jungian experience, that awoke him and made him rejoice in the fact that he was just like everyone else, very much a part of this good, good world. His eyes opened and "he saw that all things were good," even though human freedom is all too often used to desecrate and destroy what is of itself so good. Merton came to truly love the world and everyone in it. No longer did he fear or despise it.

A Life Free from Care

Freed from the ensnarements of a monastic idealism, Merton was now ready to pursue what had always been his true vocation, the uniquely free life of the hermit—the man who goes apart from the world in order that he might be at the heart of the world. At the heart of the world the hermit takes up his position as lover and prophetic voice.

Merton could speak out now and convict a sinful people, among whom he always included himself, of attempted genocide and deicide and of moving steadily toward "cosmocide," the obliteration of the entire human race. He, who had come to realize so deeply his oneness with all and rejoice in it, cried out for the black, the poor, the Chicano, his brothers and sisters in South America and South Vietnam. He cried "Peace" until his final breath, acclaiming the good in every person: Marxists and Buddhists, monastics and activists—all found their place in his catholic embrace.

Final Integration

Thomas Merton saw his life, as unique as it was, as that of Everyman. He documented it with care, even the most privileged moments of intimate love, for the sake of every man and woman. He lived out what he believed.

His final week on pilgrimage is a good example of the ability of this man of God to integrate all in a simple life of love. Early in the week he was a pious Catholic pilgrim, making his way to the tomb of Saint Thomas the Apostle, his pocket full of relics of his heavenly friends. A few days later he was walking barefoot in the shrine of the reclining Buddha, entering into one of the most moving aesthetic experiences of his life. In between he enjoyed the best hotel in Colombo, visited the bars and let scotch and jazz warm his heart.[1] "All things are yours and you are Christ's and Christ is God's."

Full Freedom of the Son of God

Thomas Merton was ready to be fully one with Christ in God. His sudden death before he completed his fifty-fourth

---

1. For a more detailed description of this experience, see chapter below, "The Legacy of Merton's Pilgrimage to India," pp. 171-73.

year we are inclined to speak of as tragic. We like to think of how much more he could have done for us, how much more he could have taught us. But if we are honest we have to admit that few of us have tried to learn all he has already taught us, for example about the dignity and freedom of the human person and the consequences of these in our lives.

Thomas Merton had completed his journey into freedom, the full freedom won for us by Christ on the cross and enjoyed only in the kingdom of God. He left behind for us more than enough to challenge us and to lead us into freedom. We cannot be truly free, he tells us, until we free in our hearts every man, woman and child in this universe, including ourselves, and then practically strive to make this a reality in everyday life.

Christ came to set us free. Merton, with his usual insight, saw this most clearly and fully; he saw all the consequences of it. Long before liberation theology became a well-known export of Latin America, Merton joined his voice to that of the South American poets as they sang of liberation, and he brought their voices into English. We American Catholics have heard Merton perhaps better than we have any Catholic voice in our times because he spoke our existential language; yet we have a ways to go in claiming our full freedom as the sons and daughters of God, of a God who came to set us free.

Growing into Compassion

Thomas Merton, the public school youth who wrote a paper on Gandhi in the 1930s, showed exceptional precocity. This paper which has unfortunately not survived for our study, is probably a truer and more authentic witness to young Merton's social concern and compassion than the fact that he kept a copy of Karl Marx's *Communist Manifesto* rather prominently displayed on his desk. But whatever seeds of compassion might have been sown by the great Indian leader, they were destined to lie dormant under a heavy layer of hedonism for some years. The exciting marches that marked life in Cambridge in the early 1930s did not benefit from Merton's participation. He was too busy partying or sleeping off the previous night's excesses.

Failure, disgrace and exile brought a wiser Merton to Columbia University, New York, in 1935. Here he did actively participate in some of the political and social demonstrations. He even joined the Communist Party for a brief period, leaving it more because of the members' lack of seriousness than because of any lack on his part. Merton was engaged with deadly earnestness (he had to struggle at least once with the urge toward suicide) in a quest for meaning, as death after death marked his young life, and he found himself more and more alone. He led his few friends, rather than being led by them, which is not to say that he did not learn from them and grow through their friendship. He was blessed with some good mentors (Mark van Doren and Dan Walsh most significantly), who did help him to grow and to find some of the answers he sought. But, as Merton himself said, it was probably minds from the past, whom he contacted through his voluminous reading, who had the greater influence on him. These are an odd mix: Gilson, Huxley, Blake, Hopkins, to name only a few. Prejudice gave way to faith. And the disciplines of faith, with its grace and hope, gradually broke open the soil for the seeds of compassion to sprout.

When in the summer of 1941 Catherine de Hueck came to the campus of Saint Bonaventure's where Merton was teaching, he was ready to hear her. At her bidding he came to Friendship House in Harlem (an outreach to the poorest and most needy started by de Hueck) for a look-see and began to give serious consideration to this as a vocation. But there was something else tugging at the young professor's heart. It was a lofty ideal which, not yet being fully understood, was able to marshall the interest of the false self in its cause. The attractive image of the contemplative saint won out over that of the self-giving apostle. An imperfect hierarchy of values still prevalent within the Catholic community undoubtedly aided in this victory. But for those who love God all things work together unto good. God would have his way with this young man, who was being seduced into a way that would prove more demanding, purifying and effective, given the special talents the Master had bestowed upon his disciple.

Thomas Merton's closest friend, Bob Lax, knew him well, and he well expressed what was going on:

When he [Merton] first got to the monastery he might have thought that he could live just a contemplative life cut off from the rest of the world. That may have been an illusion that . . . anyone could expect would soon wear off. . . . When he got back to a more universal point of view . . . that was the Merton we already knew before he got there, and it was just part of him coming back.

The Byzantine Influence

Merton did try to deny parts of himself and most of the world in these earliest monastic days. He needed a break-through to get "back to a more universal point of view." And it was, in a way, another tradition that opened the way for him: the rich Christian tradition of the Byzantine East. He had long been in touch with this tradition in various ways: the icons at Rome, his father's drawings, the Cistercian Fathers, his study of the Fathers of the Desert. In the early 1950s he had an opportunity to study the Eastern Christian Fathers more fully and reflect more profoundly on them, as he prepared and gave a course to his fellow monks. We have his notes from this course. It is here that he gets his breakthrough insight into the *theoria physike* under the tutelage of Evagrius Ponticus and Maximus the Confessor.

Merton now sees that the Christian life has three levels:

> *Bios praktikos—praxis*—the purification of the body, of the senses, of the passions—*apatheia*—the *puritas cordis* of John Cassian, something more than detachment, a positive openness to reality, to the Divine. *Theoria physike*—a spiritualized knowledge of the created, a sort of natural contemplation, which does reach on to the divine *oikonomia*, God's plan for things, and the *logoi* of things, the divine place within things. At its highest it reaches to the contemplation of the spiritual. *Theologia*—the contemplation of the Trinity without form or image.[2]

It was this understanding of *theoria physike* that enabled the zealous, ascetic, world-despising young monk to reintegrate his natural gifts and disposition toward compassion, his love

---

2. *An Introduction to Christian Mysticism—From the Apostolic Fathers to the Council of Trent.* A manuscript of lectures given at the Abbey of Gethsemani.

for all that God made, so that he could go on to become the very full and integrated person he became, a man of truest compassion. Merton himself said, "It is by *theoria* that man helps Christ redeem the *logoi* of things and restore them to Himself. . . . The *theoria* is inseparable from love and from true spiritual conduct of life."

Let me quote further from Merton's notes:

> The "will of God" is no longer a blind force plunging through our lives like a cosmic steamroller and demanding to be accepted willy nilly. On the contrary we are able to *understand* the hidden purpose of the creative wisdom and the divine mercy of God, and can cooperate with Him as a son with a loving Father. Not only that, but God Himself hands over to man, when he is thus purified and enlightened, and united with the divine will, a certain creative initiative of his own, in political life, in art, in spiritual life, in worship; man is then endowed with a *causality* of his own.[3]

Merton's "discovery" and full perception of *theoria physike* had a profound formative and liberating influence on him. This is evident in the book he produced shortly after this, *The New Man*. When Dan Walsh, who had known Merton for about twenty years, read the volume, he exclaimed, "*The New Man*—the new Merton."

But what was still perhaps too theoretical was moved forward to becoming a powerful motivating force in Merton's life through a rather Jungian experience. I will let Merton himself tell you about it, quoting from a letter addressed to Boris Pasternak:

> It is a simple enough story, but obviously I do not tell it to people—you are the fourth who knows it, and there

---

3. *Ibid.*

seems to be no point in a false discretion that might restrain me from telling you since it is clear that we have so very much in common.[4] One night [February 28, 1958] I dreamt that I was sitting with a very young Jewish girl of fourteen or fifteen, and that she suddenly manifested a very deep affection for me and embraced me so that I was moved to the depths of my soul. I learned that her name was "Proverb," which I thought very simple and beautiful. And also I thought, "She is of the race of Saint Anne." I spoke to her of her name, and she did not seem to be proud of it, because it seemed rather the other young girls mocked her for it. But I told her that it was a very beautiful name, and there the dream ended. A few days later when I happened to be in a nearby city [March 18, in Louisville], which is very rare for us, I was walking alone in the crowded street and suddenly saw that everybody was Proverb and that in all of them shone her extraordinary beauty and purity and shyness, even though they did not know who they were and were perhaps ashamed of their names—because they were mocked on account of them. And they did not know their real identity as the Child so dear to God who, from before the beginning, was playing in His sight all days, playing in the world.[5]

Merton adds with humor: "Thus you are initiated into the scandalous secret of a monk who is in love with a girl, and a Jew at that! One cannot expect much from monks these days. The heroic asceticism of the past is no more." Humor often hides truth. Merton no longer sought to be a heroic ascetic, a

---

4. That Merton could write such a line to a Russian author indicates how much he had grown in compassion. He felt a special solidarity with authors, more particularly poets, throughout the world, most especially those who spoke out for liberation.

5. *Six Letters*, pp. 11-12.

model monk, but rather a man of love, of compassion, of presence, even if the righteous were scandalized.

Merton brings this out in his more sober and less intimate account of the experience in his published journal, *Conjectures of a Guilty Bystander:*

> In Louisville, at the corner of Fourth and Walnut, in the center of the shopping district, I was suddenly overwhelmed with the realization that I loved all those people, that they were mine and I theirs, that we could not be alien to one another even though we were total strangers. It was like awaking from a dream of separateness, of spurious self-isolation in a special world, the world of renunciation and supposed holiness.[6]

This experience was not wholly new to Merton. He had had a somewhat similar or sort of initial experience almost ten years earlier, in August 1948, when he accompanied Dom Gabriel Sortais, the General of his Order, to Louisville: "I met the world and found it no longer so wicked after all. Perhaps the things I had resented about the world when I left it were defects of my own that I had projected upon it. Now, on the contrary, I found that everything stirred me with a deep and mute sense of compassion."

A Member of the Human Race

Before the experience of March 18, 1958, Merton would write of "the indignity of being a member of the human race"; afterward he would write, "It is a glorious destiny to be a member of the human race." Before he would write, "The contemplative and the Marxist have no common ground"; his

---

6. *Conjectures of a Guilty Bystander*, p. 140.

last talk would be devoted to monasticism and Marxism. He would now praise de Chardin for proclaiming the Good News in a way that was accepted by both scientists and Marxists. He would join Teilhard in his prayer, "to be widely human in my sympathies and more nobly terrestrial with my ambitions than any of the world's servants." He had entered into his depths and found One drawing all together into a common humanity, all part of one creation, all coming forth from one heart, the heart of God-Christ.

As Merton stepped further apart from the community, and in that respect further from society, to find greater freedom, he found a greater freedom to be with others. In the first days of 1964 he wrote in his journal:

> I need to find my way out of a constructed solitude which is actually the chief obstacle to realization of true solitude in openness and inner subjectivity. False solitude is built on an artificially induced awareness of unrealized possibilities of relationship with others. One prefers to keep these possibilities unrealized. (Hence, false solitude is a short-circuit to love.)[7]

Within the Community . . .

For Merton, compassion began at home. In his first year as spiritual father of the young professed, he discovered that being to them openly and lovingly was no obstacle to the solitude he sought. In 1955 he volunteered for the service of novice master and served in this office for ten years. The brethren knew that whenever they had a genuine need they could count on Father Louis to be generously available to them. Merton prized his time apart, but when he was with the

---

7. *Conjectures of a Guilty Bystander,* p. 18.

brethren he was a very cheerful and true presence. Even after he was allowed to enter fully into the life of the hermitage, he came down each week to give a talk to the brethren. Toward the end of his life, Merton spoke to the community with great frankness. He felt that the way they had been operating as a community was based on a false theology:

> We are broken persons and live in broken communities in a state of brokenness. We are alienated from ourselves and from each other. The ideal we were brought up with tended to consecrate our brokenness. We were to become united to God without any interference from one another. We went to great lengths to avoid such interference. Each sought to come to possess the ground of being, the contemplative experience of God, as if it could be his own. But the ground of being in God is totally common ground. It is a gift given to us all together, given in and through each other as members of one sole Body. If we want to be recollected, that is, centered and gathered in God, then let us drop all walls and be completely open, and we will find God in all and be centered in God, gathering, collecting all in God all the time.

. . . *and Beyond*

This openness and compassion extended beyond the community to the many who flocked to see him and to those with whom he came into contact when he went into the city. People were surprised how fully he could be with children as well as adults and enter into their personal concerns, do homework with them, read the comics and play their games.

Merton was not a southerner, but he lived half his life in the south and the plight of the blacks was very present to him.

When his consciousness expanded, he entered very fully into Martin Luther King's non-violent crusade. He put his pen at the service of the cause. Poems like "And the Children of Birmingham"[8] and "Picture of a Black Child with White Doll"[9] tear at the heart. His hopes and his frustrations with the Black Revolution are amply expressed in "Letters to a White Liberal" and "The Legend of Tucker Caliban." He felt that the Church, the Christian community as a whole and white liberals had failed the blacks, and he understood their turning to the Black Muslims.

Merton's compassion reached out to all victims: the victims of the Holocaust ("Auschwitz: A Family Camp," "A Devout Meditation in Memory of Adolf Eichmann," etc.); the victims of the bomb ("Original Child Bomb," "Target Equals City," etc.); the victims of the Vietnam war ("Notes for a Statement on Aid to Civilian War Victims in Vietnam," "Nhat Hanh is My Brother," etc.). He entered deeply into the experience of individuals: Father Max Josef Metzger ("A Martyr for Peace and Unity"); Simone Weil ("The Answer of Minerva"); Franz Jagerstatter ("An Enemy of the State").

The witness to Merton's universal compassion can be most amply authenticated from his many writings. The expressions of it are profoundly beautiful at times. But he also gives a most powerful witness to what is the ground and root of true compassion, namely a keen awareness of our common humanity, our oneness in God and God's loving design upon us, a design that calls for a unity that becomes oneness in him. There is an instinct for compassion in every human. It can be lost under overlays of selfishness and self-interest, as it was in the young Thomas Merton, or as one gives oneself to the pursuit of abstract ideals as did the young Father Louis. Yet, it will still crop out in moments of special stress, as it did for

---

8. *The Saturday Review*, August 10, 1963.

9. *The Collected Poems*, p. 636.

Merton when his brother's death called forth one of his most moving poems: "For My Brother Reported Missing in Action 1943."

True compassion, to be truly able to feel with another in all his joys and sorrows, flows only from love, a genuine love for the other. Universal compassion, an ability to feel with everyone in a personal way, can flow only from a deep love for all. Such a universal love is possible only in God. And it is only by deep experiential prayer, contemplative prayer, that we can be so grounded in God that we can give ourselves in this universal love and come to exercise and live a universal compassion.

Conversely, true prayer, contemplation, must always be one with compassion. Merton brings this out in many places:

> No man who ignores the rights and needs of others can hope to walk in the light of contemplation, because his way has turned aside from truth, from compassion, and therefore from God. The obstacle is in our "self," that is to say in the tenacious need to maintain our separate, external, egocentric will.
>
> . . . *a man cannot enter into the deepest center of himself and pass through the center into God unless he is able to pass entirely out of himself and empty himself and give himself to other people in the purity of a selfless love.*[10]

I would like to conclude this brief consideration with a prayer of Thomas Merton, a compassionate prayer:

> To be here with the silence of Sonship in my heart is to be a center in which all things converge upon you. That is surely enough for the time being. Therefore, Father, I beg you to keep me in this silence so that I may learn

---

10. *New Seeds of Contemplation*, p. 64.

from it the word of your peace and the word of your mercy and the word of your gentleness to the world. And that through me perhaps your word of peace may make itself heard where it has not been possible for anyone to hear it for a long time.[11]

11. *Conjectures of a Guilty Bystander,* p. 161.

The Merton Journals

Thomas Merton thought of himself first of all as a poet. But he is best known for his prose. And critics have agreed that some of his best prose is found in his journals. When going over the page proofs of one of them, he himself came to the same conclusion. He had decided early, after the publication of *The Ascent to Truth*, that his focus would be "not upon dogmas as such, but only on their repercussions in the life of a soul in which they begin to find concrete realization." The journal format was excellent for this.

Merton's journaling history is rather complex, as is just about everything else concerning him. He probably began writing a journal in his public school years at Oakham, but the earliest extant texts we presently have are those from the time just prior to his entering the monastic life in 1941 at the age of twenty-six. Perhaps one day some fragments of the early journals will be found, just as some fragments of his early novels, which he destroyed in 1941, have been recovered.

Beginning with the journal written in 1939, there is an almost continuous accumulation reaching to the eve of his death in December 1968. Within this collection we can distinguish four kinds of journals.

Four Kinds of Journals

There are the private journals, which Merton wrote for himself. The oldest of these are the Perry Street Journal and the Saint Bonaventure Journal, begun on October 17, 1940, which covers the time just prior to his entry into the monastery, the period when he was teaching at Saint Bonaventure's

University in Allegany, New York. On the eve of his departure for the monastery, Merton sent these journals to Mark van Doren, who in turn entrusted them to Father Irenaeus, the librarian at Saint Bonaventure's University, asking him to lock them away. Several years later, when he was working on *The Seven Storey Mountain*, Merton sent for them. Today, they, along with all the other personal journals that followed, lie in the Thomas Merton Studies Center at Bellarmine College, Louisville.

There are some gaps in this long collection, especially during the first years in the monastery until 1945,[1] when in obedience to a confessor Merton again began a serious journal. There are some journalistic entries in Merton's notebooks. These books are quite different from the journals. The journals were written in bound legers and in ink. Thus it is always evident where there have been erasures or pages removed, events which were more common in the earlier days—later Merton was content to allow the developments of his thoughts and emotions, inconsistent as they might be, to remain on record. The notebooks are spirals which allowed for pages to be easily removed without detection. These are essentially work books, gathering notes and ideas for his literary work. There is a lot of repetition in the personal journals; they reflect the daily thought of the author, which didn't necessarily alter significantly from day to day. The handwriting, too, brings us into the mood of the writer—small cramped script reveals times of greater concentration, while large flowing letters express moods of expansiveness.

Alongside the private journals, and substantially abstracted from them, is a collection of journals prepared for publication. This collection begins with *The Secular Journal* and includes *The Sign of Jonas*, a monograph called "Conjectures of a Guilty

---

1. Some early monastic journal entries have been found in the Columbia University Archives and will be included in the published journals.

Bystander," the book, *Conjectures of a Guilty Bystander, A Vow of Conversation,* and the beginnings of a sequel to this last work.

Besides these extracted journals there are several journals which Merton specifically wrote for publication. There is the very short *Day of a Stranger,* the fascinatingly interesting *Woods, Shores, Desert* and *The Asian Journal.* Part of his final journal was also published as *Thomas Merton in Alaska.*

Finally there are a couple of very special journals of which we will speak later.

Let us look at these journals in chronological order.

The Secular Journal

The first abstracted journal, which was published under the title, *The Secular Journal,* was prepared by Merton in 1940-41. It was abstracted from three journals: the Perry Street Journal, the Saint Bonaventure Journal, and an earlier one which is lost.[2] Merton first called this edited journal, "The Cuban Journal." The central part recounts his trip to Cuba, where he had some profound experiences in faith—the *Credo* came alive for him and he came to know Nuestra Senora de Cobreces. The journal opens on Perry Street, October 1, 1939, with much talk of poetry, literature and war. He explores a Franciscan vocation with sad consequences. The move to Saint Bonaventure's comes after the springtime pilgrimage to Cuba. It is from the University that Merton makes his first visit to Gethsemani, discovers Harlem and visits Our Lady of the Valley, the Cistercian monastery in Rhode Island (now Spencer, Massachusetts). In the final entry he writes: "Today I think: should I be going to Harlem, or to the Trappists?" and concludes: "I shall speak to one of the Friars." The entry is dated November 27, 1941. Two weeks later Merton was on his way to Gethsemani.

---

2. A transcript of the journal he kept while in Cuba in the spring of 1940, parts of which appeared in *The Secular Journal,* has been recently discovered.

The flavor of *The Secular Journal* is quite different from the
surviving personal journal and from the account in *The Seven
Storey Mountain*. That is perhaps because it is twice edited.
Before he boarded the train for Gethsemani, Merton sent the
manuscript to Catherine de Hueck Doherty. It was his hope
that she might one day get it published and use the income for
her Catholic Action work, to which he had felt so drawn. It
was to make up for the car he had promised her but would
now never be able to deliver. More importantly, it would help
her to understand his decision. From this time Merton called
the manuscript, "Journal for Catherine." It was fourteen years
later, when the journalist had attained worldwide fame that
Catherine approached him about publishing the journal. In
1955 Merton found himself subject to the censors and superiors of his Order. A long and painful struggle ensued. Some
rather melodramatic letters were written about the starving
poor who would be fed and housed with the royalties. At one
point the Abbot of Gethsemani agreed to repay the five hundred dollars advance Catherine had already collected for the
journal's publication. In the end permission for publication
was granted, but further editing was required, and it was to
be made very clear that the journal was written before Merton
entered the monastery. Hence the very specific name: *The
Secular Journal*. Merton had offered others: Diary of Young
Thomas Merton, Reflections of Yesteryear, News of an Ancient Battle, Meditations of a Young Moose, To Hell and Back
with Uncle Lou, and The Grass Was Greener in the Late
Thirties.

The Sign of Jonas

Merton's next abstracted journal has remained one of his
most popular books. *The Seven Storey Mountain* allowed only
about forty pages to describe Merton's life as a monk. They

were tantalizing. Everyone who read the best-selling autobiography wanted to know more about life inside the walls. They wanted to know how this wild young man actually fared as a monk. *The Sign of Jonas* is the nearest thing to a sequel to the autobiography. It stays close to his personal journal and therefore has a refreshing actuality, as it follows him through his monastic life from December 10, 1946 until July 4, 1952.

This was a very significant period for Merton as a monk, as a man and as a writer. He moved on to solemn vows, his final consecration as a monk, a commitment he was never tempted to go back on, at least in regard to the essence—being a monk. But it contained an element, the vow of stability, which he perceived as the belly of the whale, the paradox, that carried this prophet—for every monk is a prophet—resolutely in the opposite direction of the one in which he wanted to go. Greater solitude in many forms constantly lured him, yet his vow carried him ever more deeply into the life of a community.

Merton's manhood received its crown in this period in his ordination to the priesthood. He sensed deeply that this was what he had been created to be: a priest of Jesus Christ, one with Christ in his priesthood. He would live out this calling very personally and deeply.

The period also saw Merton's only prolonged period of writer's block. In the end he broke through, not without some serious psychosomatic problems. In completing *The Ascent to Truth* though, Merton came to realize, as I noted above, that that kind of theological writing was not for him. He found his genre, and it never abandoned him from that time on.

The Sign of Jonas is rich in homey monastic details of the commonplace. This is part of its attraction. Although it was not written as a "spiritual journal," it has some beautiful and profound insights. Above all it reveals a very real and human man-made-monk. It is Merton at his best if not yet at his maturist and most integrated. That would come.

Conjectures of a Guilty Bystander

The next abstracted journal is already a giant step in that direction. Merton's long-time friend and literary agent, Naomi Burton Stone, has declared this her favorite, and she has a very dog-eared copy to prove her assertion. *Conjectures of a Guilty Bystander* is worth going back to again and again.

Merton lays out the facts concerning the book in the preface:

> The material is taken from notebooks I have kept since 1956.[3] Though they are personal and conversational and represent my own verson of the world, these entries are not of the intimate and introspective kind that go to make up a spiritual journal. There is certainly nothing private or confidential here. . . . Maybe the best way to look at this book is to say that it consists of a series of sketches and meditations, some poetic, some literary, others historical and even theological, fitted together in a spontaneous, informal philosophic scheme in such a way that they react upon each other. The total result is a personal and monastic meditation, a testimony of Christian reflection in the mid-twentieth century, a confrontation of twentieth-century questions in the light of monastic commitment.

The journal reveals the rich variety of Merton's world, a cosmic person, full of tradition, poverty and compassion. Russian mystics, space travellers and oppressed blacks follow each other on the pages. Heisenberg and John of the Cross are seen to walk hand in hand. At times it is a bit jolting. Merton dispatches of his reactions to President John Kennedy's murder in a couple of paragraphs (one can sense the great emotion

---

3. This is being written in November 1965, though the material used leaves off at the end of 1963.

beneath the words) and goes on with some rather abstruse albeit important theologizing with Anselm of Bec. Merton, seeing things from a vantage point shared with Saint Peter— for the monk is the latter-day upside-down martyr—turns the world right side up. "Materialism" is seen as "the opium of the people." The objectivity of conventual physics is as much a myth as the sun going around the earth.

Conjectures of a Guilty Bystander is rich, too rich to be summarized.

It was actually preceded by another "Conjectures of a Guilty Bystander." In an author's note prefaced to this eighty-three-page monograph, Merton tells the story:

> The following pages are excerpts from notebooks and journals written about 1958-1961. They were typed up with a view to publication. On reflection, the idea of publication in this particular form was felt to be impractical at the present time. The book was abandoned when about half stencilled. The stencils remained on the shelf for some time. Before destroying them, I thought we might run off twenty-five copies for friends. Some of this material should eventually reappear in another form, and a book is planned with the same title. It will however be very different from this.

The note is dated April 1965. Most of the material that is found in this monograph is in fact found in *Conjectures of a Guilty Bystander*, though some beautiful pages have been left out, most notably the entry on Cardenal. Almost all of the forty entries have a political note about them, whether they speak of Moscow or the Congo, Central America or native Kentucky, where Happy Chandler stands on the steps of the Gethsemani guesthouse and speaks of his "young friend, Thomas Merton." The tone is set in the first entry: "The real way to spiritual renewal is precisely where you would least expect it: in the field of political life. *It is here that all the crucial struggles and temptations of our time have to be faced.*"

A copy of this monograph can be found in the Merton Collection at Boston College.

A Vow of Conversation

While *Conjectures of a Guilty Bystander* was making its slow journey toward publication, Merton set about producing another abstracted journal for publication. This one he called *A Vow of Conversation*. It covers Merton's last days in the community, his last days as novice master, his gradual move toward the full eremitical life. The first entry is New Year's Eve 1963; the last—September 9, 1965— written a couple of weeks after he had left office and moved up to the hermitage on the Feast of Saint Bernard, August 20.

It is definitely a continuation of *Conjectures of a Guilty Bystander*, yet like *The Sign of Jonas* it is closer to life. The little boy is still there: flying kites, sliding in the snow, tearing his pants on barbed wire; yet the poet catches beauty and expresses it in words that no child could ever find. And the theologian knowledgeably hobnobs with Bultmann ("Fantastically good"), Sartre, and Simone Weil, while the literator evaluates the contribution of Merleau-Ponty. What we see most vulnerably exposed in this journal is a hurt Merton, a misunderstood monk, a feared because powerful writer, who is still struggling with basic questions as to the proper stance for him, even while he occasionally lashes out with masterly irony in the direction of authority.

The polished typescript was completed not long before Merton's final journey East. Merton sent it to his agent and friend, Naomi Burton Stone, with a note acknowledging that he had been a bit too harsh in his reactions to Dom James, his abbot, and others and encouraging her to use her blue pencil liberally. Mrs. Stone would have, had Merton been there to approve her pencilling. But providence had it otherwise. And Mrs. Stone did not feel free to change the text of the deceased monk. She thought it should be published as it stood. In the end she was out-voted by the other two members of the Merton Legacy Trust and the typescript remained unpublished for many years. On the title page Merton had typed "for Doubleday," the publisher of *Conjectures of a Guilty Bystander*. On the copy in the Merton Center at Columbia University we find a note from Sister Therese Lentfoehr: "He *certainly meant this to be published!*"

An Incomplete Journal

We have a final piece of abstracted journal, which is still in an initial state of being abstracted. In September 1967, Merton began to dictate a manuscript drawing on his 1966 journal. The point he makes in a note he prefaces to the text, I think is important to keep in mind when reading not only Merton's journals but also the biographies written about him:

On this tape I want to read some sections from a journal kept in 1966, a journal about what goes on in a hermitage, to a great extent. The best thing that goes on in a hermitage is nothing, and so you can't put nothing down. So therefore whatever is put down is usually the second best: that is to say, things about reading, things about work, things about messing around, and also occasional visits of people. One thing that this journal may give the impression of is that there are constant visitors, but in point of fact this is misleading, because I have a tendency to put down visitors on account of the fact that that means something had happened and something is to be put down. But as I said, the best of the journal is not put down because it is what does not happen.

Later on in the typescript we are given a little more insight into Merton's way of constructing these abstracted journals for publication: "Now I am going to cheat a little bit here and insert some brand new material that I am just thinking of at the moment, that is to say October 5, 1967, which is not in the sequence of the journal, but which fits in with it, I believe. It just happens this morning that I have been reading . . ."

Finally, in the last pages of this beginning—fifty-one pages, ending with the entry for April 2—Merton is preparing to enter the hospital and he waxes a bit nostalgic. "Certainly the spirit of the community [at Gethsemani] is good and the place is blessed. There are good men here. It is a sincere and excellent community." Then he goes on to speak of individuals, coming to Dom James: "Dom James, with all his limitations and idiosyncrasies, has done much good in this community just by stubbornly holding everything together. He too is an extraordinary person, many-sided, baffling, often very irritating, a man of enormous, stubborn will, and who honestly in his own way really seeks to be an instrument of God. And in the end that is what he turned out to be, whether for good or for otherwise." Merton goes on to express his gratitude for his gradual entrance into a more completely eremitical life, concluding: "But there are greater gifts even than this, and God knows best what is for my good and for the good of the whole world. The best is what he wills."

It would have been most interesting if Merton had continued this editing of his journal. For it was just after this time while he was in the hospital that he met the young nurse with whom he shared a very deeply felt experience of love. How would he have treated this very personal and significant relationship and all the impact it had on his monastic life for some months and afterward in a selective and carefully edited journal?

I mentioned above that there are a couple of special journals. These are two journals Merton wrote in 1966 for this young nurse, whom his biographer refers to as S. (and so shall I). The *Midsummer Diary: Piece of a Small Journal. Or an Account of How I Once Again Became Untouchable*, which was composed between June 15 and 25, 1966, is typed rather than handwritten and was delivered to S. on the latter date. *Retrospect* was written for her a little later. In his personal journal, Merton notes that these accounts written for S. give "a more balanced view" of the affair. In his biography, *The Seven Mountains of Thomas Merton*, Michael Mott handles this whole matter with delicacy and balance. I will add nothing further here. An inventory of Merton's journals would not be complete, though, without mention of these two significant pieces.

Journals Written for Publication

Finally, we must look at the journals that Merton specifically wrote in view of publication.

The first was written in May of 1965 in response to a request. Merton had a special affection for Latin America, a growing interest in its poets and in its political affairs. When a South American editor asked him to describe a typical day in his life he responded with *Day of a Stranger*. The Spanish word *extrano* (stranger) is not far from the "bystander" we know in English. This one-day journal was written in the period when Merton was moving more and more toward the hermitage. The piece was published in English two years later in *The Hudson Review* and in 1981 in an attractive booklet. All the threads of Merton's day from 2:15 A.M. until night are woven into a rich prose poem, which makes us realize how much peace and war, ecology and desecration were a part of the fabric of the life of this concerned "stranger" whom we know as a brother.

Woods, Shore, Desert

Three years later, in the same month, under a new abbot, Merton made one of his first significant journeys. He was ostensively looking for a more remote site for his hermitage— too many were discovering the road that led up to the cement block cottage behind Gethsemani Abbey. The journey gave him an opportunity to visit admired and admiring friends, the Trappistines of Redwoods Abbey in northern California and the Benedictines of Christ in the Desert in New Mexico. The journal, entitled, *Woods, Shore, Desert*, opens with notes for the conferences he will be giving to the nuns, continues with an entry written on the first day of his trip, May 6, and goes on to May 30, a final entry written some time after his return to Gethsemani. This journal is Merton near the end without the ponderous weight of Asia. It is Merton the poet and artist.

Merton has become an integrated mystic and conveys his cosmic and earthly contemplation in a way it can best be conveyed: through poetics and artistry. For the most part the text is poetry, prose poetry, pure poetry. We delight in it. Then suddenly we come upon seemingly bizarre passages about the comic art of Molière, and we realize that we are far from grasping the full scope of Merton's luxuriant and diverse personality.

The breadth of the context within which Merton expresses the creation is indicated already in the few quotations in the prelude, which include the *Astavahra Gita*, a Russian Orthodox (Yelchaninov), Paschal, Saint Bernard and Martin Luther King, among others. The text will go on to quote A. Stern, Unamuno, Theophane the Recluse, Francis Ponge, Lu T'ung, Krishna, Daumal, Poulet, Sidi Abdesalam, and Hisamatsu.

At this point, we wonder, where is Merton in his personal journey toward freedom? We read: "Too much conformity to roles. Is it just a matter of brushing up the roles and adjusting the roles? A role is not necessarily a vocation. One can be alienated by role filling." And then: "Two daiquiris in the airport bar. Impression of relaxation. Even only in the airport, a sense of recovering something of myself that has been lost. On a little plane to Eureka, the same sense of ease, of openness."

Yet, Merton remains the monk, concerned about monasticism—authentic monasticism, a monasticism of being: "Fatal emphasis [in the monastic life] on acquiring something. . . . Baloney!" But, being in relation. The social concern, the ecological concern constantly crop out:

> In our monasticism we have been content to find our way to a kind of peace, a simple undisturbed thoughtful life. And this certainly is good, but is it good enough? I, for one, realize now I need more. . . . There is need of effort, deepening, change and transformation. . . . I do have to break with an accumulation of inertia, waste, foolishness, rot, junk, a great need of clarification of mindfulness, or rather effort, need to push on to the great doubt. Need for the Spirit.

Merton places himself in the context of the Hindu states of life. Not *Brahmacharya* (the young man learning chastity); not *Grhastha* (the husband fathering children); nor the ultimate *Sanyasa* (the life of total renunciation), but *Vanaprastha* (the solitary life in the forest). "My present life. A life of privacy and of quasi-retirement. Is there one more stage?" In the end Merton finds himself and true freedom: "I am the utter poverty of God. I am His emptiness, littleness, nothingness, lostness. When this is understood my life is His freedom, the self-emptying of God in me is the fullness of grace. A love for God that knows no reason because he is the fullness of grace. A love for God that knows no reason because He is God; a love without measure."

The Asian Journal

Five months later, on October 15, as his plane lifts off from San Francisco, Merton begins a new journal for publication, "Asian Notes." He will never complete it. At the same time he continues his personal journal of the period to which he has given the interesting title, "The Hawke's Dream." And he will be keeping a pocket notebook for cryptic notes, various jottings and poetic inspirations. From these three sources, the published *Asian Journal* was produced. In "Asian Notes" Merton had put texts that interested him on one side of the notebook and his journaling on the other. The editors brought this into a coherent text, used the private journal to fill in some gaps and from the cryptic pocket notebook rescued the delightful "Kandy Express." It was a monumental labor of love.

An edited and in some part collated work, *The Asian Journal* doesn't have the literary perfection of *Woods, Shore, Desert,* but it does have the same staggering richness of content, blown large. And it has passages that will be forever classic Merton. The conjunction of the very Catholic pilgrimage to Saint Thomas in Madras, the very-much-of-this-world pilgrimage to the bars of Colombo, and the barefoot approach to the Buddha at Polonnaruwa tells us, if we listen, to what an extent this very human mystic did get it all together and experienced a unity in all as coming incessantly from the one Source of all.[4]

---

4. See chapter below "The Legacy of Merton's Pilgrimage to India."

The Circular Letters

It was for Christmas in 1966 that Thomas Merton resorted for the first time to the use of a circular letter.[1] As he explained to the recipients, he used it "to provide some way of answering all those I cannot answer personally." The response was in fact quite favorable. Probably many felt that a circular letter is better than no letter at all. And Merton's richly personal style was not lacking in these relatively short and quite newsy epistles.

With his recipients' encouragement, Merton went on to write twelve more circular letters in the course of the two years that remained of his life. These letters have a particular value and importance. In them we find summed up those items Merton considered most significant during the last two years of his life—the things he wanted to share with those whom he considered in a special way his friends and companions on life's journey. It might then be profitable to survey the contents of these thirteen circular letters to friends.

Christmas, 1966

As I already mentioned, the first was sent out by Merton at Christmastime 1966. In two short years he would be dead and buried by the side of the Abbey Church, the completion of whose renovation he announces as proximate in this letter. In

---

1. There were actually a few earlier general letters: one to "high school students" dating from 1963, a Christmas letter sent out in 1965, and a "Statement to Friends" sent out earlier in 1966 to allay rumors. The regular practice or series, however, begins at the end of 1966.

the letter Merton describes his current existence as "a marginal life in solitude." It opens with a curious account of a phone call Frank Sheed received in London at four in the morning from a pseudo-Merton. The burden of the letter is to explain his inability to write to all personally and at the same time to defend his continued production as an author in spite of his move into solitude. The reasons for acting contrary to what is "favored offically by monks" are "that if you know something and do not share it, you lose your own knowledge of it" and that there are "some obligations to take up a position on this or that moral issue of general urgency."

We may or may not agree with Merton's reasons, but we cannot help but be touched by the down-to-earth humility that marks this letter. In commenting on Sheed's experience he says: "There are people around who are crazy enough to think that if they pretend they are Thomas Merton it means something." Speaking of the development of his thought and insight, he says: "I don't know the answers, but I have some questions I'd like to share with you. . . . But now I am beginning to wonder if I even know the questions."

His concern for issues was very real and practical. This comes out in his request that those who would like to send him something would send it to the Quakers to relieve those suffering on both sides of the Arab-Israeli war. "I am trying not to appear to take either side in this senseless conflict, rooted in hate and misunderstanding and fomented by power politicians in the 'big' powers. But the refugees and homeless are refugees nevertheless, regardless of the merits and demerits of their 'side.' "

The only item of "news" in this letter is the announcement of the passing of Victor Hammer. The brief, touching eulogy notes that Victor was painting the resurrection when he fell ill.

It is evident in the closing remarks that Merton had not intended this to be the beginning of a series of such letters, but that he wanted it to be at most an annual thing, for he wishes his readers "a good summer"—it is December when he is writing.

Septuagesima, 1967

Less than two months later he is again writing,[2] opening his letter with: "Several wrote that they liked my mimeographed Christmas letter and urged me to go on mimeographing more often." Merton hardly needed encouragement.

This letter is largely inspired by the event of Father Charles Davis' leaving the Catholic Church. It is strong and reasonable and a powerful witness to faith. Merton is sympathetic and compassionate—and urges this same response on the part of his readers— admitting candidly that "being a Catholic and being a monk have not always been easy." He speaks very frankly about his own reaction to all of this: "There have been bad days when I might have considered doing what Fr. Davis has done. In actual fact I have never seriously considered leaving the Church, and though the question of leaving the monastic state *has* presented itself, I was not able to take it seriously for more than five or ten minutes."

Merton found his solution partly in Pascal: "He recognized the destructiveness of his own inner demon in time and knew enough to be silent and to believe. And to love." And even more in a spirit of gratitude. "I owe too much to the Church and to Christ . . . the grace, love and infinite mercy of Christ in His Church." He acknowledged that he could be as unreasonable and intolerant as any hierarch in the Church might be. He knew his need to be forgiven and the evangelical command not to judge and to forgive. "By God's grace I remain a Catholic, a monk and a hermit. I have made commitments which are unconditional and cannot be taken back."

---

2. This letter is dated Septuagesima Sunday, which was February 11, 1967, but the text shows that Merton was writing prior to his birthday on January 31.

The other element in this letter is that of friendship. "More and more I see the meaning of my relationship with all of you, and the value of the love that unites us, usually unexpressed." He talks about the difficulties of keeping up correspondence and of visits. "But there is such a thing as being united in prayer, or even thought and desire (if you can't pray). . . .[3] The main thing is that we desire good for each other and seek within the limits of our power to obtain for each other what we desire."

Lent, 1967

Five weeks later Merton is again composing a letter. His stock of the last one is gone, and Easter is still four weeks away. Moreover he is about to go into the hospital for an operation on his elbow for bursitis and will have difficulty typing, so he is stocking up on a new letter. We see from this that Merton used these periodical letters to respond to mail as it came in day after day.

The burden of this letter is to respond, and respond strongly, to a couple of objections he had received in regard to *Conjectures of a Guilty Bystander*. Some readers had felt he was too negative in regard to technology.

Merton makes it clear that what he was aiming at is the "myth that technology infallibly makes everything in every way better for everybody." The reality is that in our technological world we have wonderful means for keeping people alive and for killing people off, and they both go together. "We rush in and save lives from tropical diseases, then we come along with napalm and burn up the people we have saved." Merton was writing at the time of the Vietnam War.

Merton saw the potential of technology and the obligation that flows from that:

---

3. Remember that Merton's corresponding friends included an immensely wide and varied audience, hence the parenthesis.

Technology could indeed make a much better world for
millions of human beings. . . . We have an absolute
obligation to use the means at our disposal to keep
people from living in utter misery and dying like flies.
The fact is that we are not doing this. If we did use our
immense technological expertise we could easily feed
everyone and get the *twelve percent* who live in shanty
towns into human habitation. Instead of creating work,
labor-saving technology has left more and more unem-
ployed and in abject poverty, enriching the few who
have the capital.

The problem lies in the fact that human needs have been
politicized. Merton is extremely harsh in his judgment of
Johnson's great "war on poverty": "It is a sheer insult to the
people living in our eastern Kentucky mountains. All the attention and money are going . . . to enrich the big corporations that
are making higher profits now than they ever did before." The
answer lies in freeing technology from profit and power and
using it for the people. Merton points to Church documents:
Mater et Magistra and *Gaudium et Spes*. He took the documents
very seriously. His social concern, even though he admits to his
letter being a bit of a "tirade" with some "caricatures," flows
from the teaching of the Church. He was a Catholic who really
took the gospel and the Church seriously and not selectively.

As he moves toward a concluding paragraph, Merton says
that he "thought it was worthwhile to make this point clear."
I agree with him. We do need to hear today what he wrote
years ago.

His final paragraph looks to the coming feast of Easter.
Christians must not use this feast "to canonize earthly injustice
and despair." The power and presence of the resurrection is
with us now to give us hope and enable us to make a difference
that flows out of an "entire and total commitment to the law
of Christ which is the law of love."

Easter, 1967

Merton's Easter letter opens with the plaint, "Answering letters individually gets to be more and more of a problem." To underline the point, he goes on to detail the work lying on his desk waiting to be done—it takes half a page to do this. The conclusion is that carrying on an ordinary friendly correspondence is normally just out of the question. "The life of a writing hermit is certainly not one of lying around in the sun or of pious navel gazing." Yet, Merton strongly affirms that for him meditation "is always the first thing of all, because without it the rest becomes meaningless."

Merton goes on to recommend a new British publication, *Theoria to Theory*, even giving the address to subscribe. This magazine was to foster a dialogue between theologians and contemplatives on the one hand and scientists, philosophers and humanists on the other, a dialogue which greatly interested Merton. He would, of course, make his own contribution to the journal, though he had little opportunity in the time that remained to do much.

This shorter letter concludes with a very rich meditation on the meaning of Easter, which evokes Blake's "Tyger, Tyger burning bright." Faith cannot end in response to statements or systems; it has to be a response to persons and above all to *the* Person. We have to surrender our ego-mastery to his mastery. "There is no joy but in the victory of Christ over death in us: And all love that is valid has something of that victory. . . . Easter celebrates the victory of love over everything."

Pentecost, 1967

Merton again takes up his pen at Pentecost, and joy erupts in the first sentence. The man who had first put him on the path to Gethsemani and made the priesthood possible for him,

Dan Walsh, has just been ordained to the priesthood. Merton
and many others saw the ordaining of this elderly professor
of philosophy without a lot of formalities as a sign that the
Church was indeed moving in the direction they hoped for—
"less systematic and less rigid . . . something that leaves room
for a more charismatic kind of religion." Merton went into
Louisville to concelebrate with Fr. Walsh at the Carmel, a great
celebration, "a great deal of very authentic joy."

The feast invited Merton to comment on the widespread
desire for the *experience* of God and the Pentecostal movement.
He was completely in support of these things though he for
his part "always tended more toward a deepening of faith in
solitude and . . . not seek special experiences."

Merton saw this spiritual awakening as part of a larger
coming into fuller humanity, a liveliness that sought greater
participation in life.

Merton spoke of a couple of the good signs of monastic
renewal that were taking place: Dom Jacques Winandy's eremitical colony in Vancouver and a simplified foundation un-
dertaken by some Cistercians on the Island of Bornholm in
Denmark. But we cannot rest on what others are doing: "As
for me, the job of renewal boils down to the conversion of my
own life."

Advent-Christmas, 1967

There would be a considerable lapse of time before Merton
again composed a missive for his friends. "This year has gone
by fast. . . ."

It had its sorrows. Two Columbia friends died, Ad Rein-
hardt and John Slate. They are touchingly eulogized with the
concluding thought, "Both died of heart attacks, and both
were about my age. So if I suddenly follow their example I will
be the last one to be surprised." Prophetic words!

His community has moved into their renovated church, and Merton is happy with it: "The church of Gethsemani is an inspiring place to worship."

But he is not happy about everything. He goes on to explain again the need of these circular letters and then speaks about the many invitations he receives for lectures, all of which he has to refuse. He says, "For me it would be a waste of time. I have better ways of communicating with the outside world." I think we are inclined to agree with the judgment but also to be suspicious as to whether Merton really held it. The fact is that at this time he had to refuse all invitations; Dom James would not allow any such exits. A few months later when he had a new abbot, he was soon moving about and giving lectures.

Merton gives a rather shrewd appraisal of monastic renewal. In the long run he is hopeful. The renewal is going to move slowly. He likes what he sees among the young. The older "have had it." His concern is for the middle group: "They have a fifty-fifty chance, maybe." In fact, things haven't worked out quite that well for them. As he goes on, Merton sounds almost callous in the way he endorses what might be God's pruning plans.

He then whirls through a whole series of opinions on the Hippies, Johnson, the Beatles, LSD, the peace movement, ending with his sharpest words on the Vietnam War: "It is one of the greatest and most stupid blunders in American history, and the results are a disgrace." The letter ends with a call to live out of faith and love, a real struggle. But that is what Christmas is all about, this Advent-Christmas letter says.

New Year's, 1968

Shortly after there was a New Year's Letter—the year Merton would never finish on earth. Besides the need to answer many letters, Merton had a special reason to write this one, and two special matters to deal with. The first matter and the reason was a *National Catholic Reporter* article by Coleman McCarthy, a former member of the Gethsemani daughter-house in Conyers, Georgia. McCarthy had quoted Merton in ways that gave misleading impressions. The second matter was the forthcoming abbatial election.

Announcing Dom James' retirement, Merton acknowledges the abbot's contribution, especially in regard to the acceptance of the eremitic life into the Order, the life the abbot was soon to embrace, but also for "all the other ways he built up our community and provided for it over more than eighteen years as abbot."

In speaking of both of these matters, Merton gives us his criteria for true monastic renewal, a concern that loomed large for him at that time. It "must focus on the reality of the monastic vocation to inner freedom, to creativity, to dialogue with other contemplative traditions." The new abbot was to be one who would "help us find creative solutions," who would lead the monks "fully in line with the charism of the monastic life and . . . enable us to fulfill our real function in the Church and the world today." For Merton the monastic life was never a fully enclosed thing, divorced from the Church and the world, even though apart. He recognized the difficulties, the challenge, the need for a creativity. He agreed with McCarthy in many ways, but had a fuller, deeper, richer perspective.

And yet a deep current of traditionalism flowed in this monk, who underwent a rigorous Trappist formation in the 1940s. It crops out here in a promise to offer Mass on the Epiphany for the recipients of this letter, "my dear friends, near and far, new and old, including all of you whom I have never met except through the courtesy of the U.S. mail—and the monastery mail room."

Pre-Lent, 1968

As he opens his Pre-Lent Letter, he speaks at greater length of his correspondents: students, those in the peace movement, men in service in Vietnam, fans, critics, inquirers and those asking favors: "I am tempted to follow the example of Edmund Wison with his famous printed card, on which he simply checks off the item he cannot supply." He is happy about the abbatial election of Fr. Flavian, "a young monk who, I would say, represents a middle position between conservatism and wild innovation."

Merton then turns his attention to those who have left the monasteries—their numbers were growing—especially those who were seeking to continue their basic monastic calling in some new and simpler way. He wanted a real dialogue between them and the communities. He also wanted nuns to have an opportunity to live the eremitical life.

In this letter Merton marks the passing of another friend, "one of my oldest and best friends from Columbia," Sy Freedgood. It was Sy who brought the Hindu monk, Bramachari into Merton's life, an important influence in Merton's finding his own vocation.

A new abbot—has the scene changed? Merton again explores the idea of going on lecturing tours. Again we wonder if he protests too much. He did not yet know the freedom and responsibility he was to find under Fr. Flavian in regard to such matters. He speaks of two forthcoming books, which he sees will be misunderstood: *Cables to the Ace*—"may baffle a lot of readers . . . obscure and indirect . . . perhaps some of the younger ones will intuitively pick up some of the shorthand"—and *Faith and Violence*—"It will make a lot of people very mad." He concludes: "I have already said more than I intended."

Easter, 1968

The Easter Letter of 1968 is written early, in fact a couple of weeks early, as the next letter indicates. There is snow on the ground. Requests are pouring in for him to come and talk (no wonder, after all the hints in his previous letters!) but all "have to be refused."

The bulk of this letter is taken up with a rather heavy but compassionate consideration of the question of the validity of the religious life. Merton speaks of his coming to Gethsemani. He found a life that did have "something warped and inhuman about it . . . hard, even unreasonably hard . . . with a theology that is in some ways pathological." "We carry deep wounds that will prevent us from ever forgetting it." This is a statement that should be kept in mind when looking at the later Merton. It should not be forgotten when dealing with older persons who find it hard to move with some of the changes.

This negative side, though, has its counterbalance. For one thing, the basic values of medieval monasticism retain their validity. And one has to admit that "the injustices, the distortions, the inhumanities of secular life are incomparably worse (so we feel)." But most important, there was a sense of really being called by God. Gethsemani was for Merton a "sign of Christ." "Though we may have shed one illusion after another and gone deeper and deeper into the radical questioning of our life and our vocation, we have nevertheless elected to stay with it because we have continued to believe that this was what God asked of us." Merton admits that he would be slow at this point to write extolling the monastic vocation as it then was, or to encourage anyone to enter. He rather points to the eschatological life proclaimed by Paul. When we have grown we sometimes forget that others are not yet where we are, that they still need and can profit by the things that helped us get where we are, even though now we can see their flaws and no longer can be helped by them.

Before concluding the letter, Merton lists (with addresses) some of the less accessible journals where his writings can be found: *The Catholic Worker, Monastic Studies, Unicorn Journal, Poetry* and the *Sewanee Review*.

Paschal Time, 1968

The next letter, dated Paschal Time 1968, again marks a personal loss for Merton. This time it is his nearest living relative, his father's sister, the aunt who visited him at Gethsemani in 1964. She died in a shipwreck, losing her own life after giving heroic help to others.

But this personal loss is overshadowed by another loss that was both personal and national, if not universal—the tragic martyrdom of Martin Luther King. King was scheduled soon to visit Merton at Gethsemani for a retreat. In spite of his deep feelings about the oppression of blacks in this country, Merton keeps to rather sober and measured tones here. It is the measure of his grief and sense of loss for a people and a nation. It was perhaps tempered by the fact that Johnson had decided not to run for another term.

Merton devotes a long paragraph to speak about how important the dialogue between Christianity and Asian religions is. He has just been asked to do the introduction for an important book on Zen Buddhism. He has been lecturing to the monks on Sufism. There is depth to be found in these religions, the kind of depth Merton sought in coming to Catholicism. The renewal would be sadly mistaken if it sought to be relevant rather than deep. With Pentecost approaching, Merton summons the Church to be "in every sense prophetic and eschatological: a sign of Christ which is at once a sign of supreme hope and a sign of contradiction."

Summer, 1968

It is not surprising that the next letter, Midsummer 1968, again features an assassination. Merton reflects on the murder of Robert Kennedy on June 5 in the context of the sickness of a society, our society with its growing tendency to harm and to destroy the very things we claim to need and admire.

In the face of this, Merton felt it necessary to defend or at least explain the act of Dan and Phil Berrigan in their "extreme" and "shocking" destruction of draft cards. At this distance the juxtaposition seems almost ludicrous—that some people could be more upset about the destruction of draft cards than they were about the destruction of the lives of the draftees, sent to die in a meaningless war. For some people law and order is more important than life itself. Merton felt that his own position was "somewhere in between." He opposed the draft as needless and in fact being used for aggression. But he thought that it should be abolished "by the normal political means."

These circular letters were the only way Merton could respond to the mounting volume of mail. As he says at the beginning of this Midsummer Letter, in them he tries to answer some of the questions that have been addressed to him, though he feels he has "expressed too many opinions about everything, and I wish I could really be silent on controversial events." He is tired of "clarifying." His stance *is* clear: "I am against war, against violence, against violent revolution, for peaceful settlement of differences, for non-violence but nevertheless radical change." The gospel commitment has political implications. One cannot be for Christ and espouse a political cause that implies callous indifference to the needs of millions of human beings and even cooperates in their destruction.

In the opening paragraph of this letter, Merton again speaks of refusing invitations. This is a little bit less than candid. He speaks of being "quite busy during May" but says nothing of his trip to California and Arizona. No mention is made of the plans under way for the long and final journey East.

Fall, 1968

He comes clean in the Fall Letter: "I'd better make the whole thing clear." He outlines the plans that have been made: meetings to attend, monasteries to visit. And he expects more invitations. The reasons for all this, in spite of previous statements, are "the crucial importance of the time, the need for monastic renewal, the isolation and helplessness of our Asian monasteries, their constant appeals for help." Certainly, very valid reasons. We can add to them his personal hope "to get in contact with Buddhist monasticism and see something of it first hand." A couple of times he expresses his concern about rumors and adds rather naively, "Needless to say, this is not anything unusual in the monastic life."

The trip is to be "absolutely non-political." He will not go to Vietnam in spite of earlier hopes and plans. Merton questions whether the time for protests and petitions has now passed. For him it has. There is a certain completing about this September letter. There will be another from Asia, a much longer letter than any of these and more formal—not quite the same friendly missive these have been.

The Final Letter

The final circular was penned by Merton in New Delhi on November 9, a month before his death, two months into his journey. Unlike the others, it is not a reply to mail, for he has not been getting much as he has moved along.

There were concerns and rumors that Merton would stay in Asia, that he would become a Buddhist. There is no indication of that in this letter. Indeed, it gives witness to the opposite: "I also hope I can bring back to my monastery something of the Asian wisdom with which I am fortunate to be in contact. . . . In my contacts with these new friends I also feel consolation in my own faith in Christ and His indwelling presence."

The letter includes many colorful vignettes of India and Bangkok, though the main part is a report on his visit with the Dalai Lama, a monk who evidently made a strong impression on him. On the whole he found that his "contacts with Asian monks have been very fruitful and rewarding." He had met a Cambodian Buddhist monk, an English Buddhist monk and a Tibetan. "It is invaluable to have direct contact with people who have really put in a lifetime of hard work in training their minds and liberating themselves from passion and illusion." The Dalai Lama had asked Merton if there were possibilities of deep mystical life in our monasteries. Merton replied, "Well, that is what they are supposed to be for, but many seem to be interested in something else." It is with this sobering thought and challenge that Merton leaves us.

This very rapid survey of thirteen rich letters hardly gives a summary view of their varied contents. But they do demonstrate the extent and the depth of Merton's concerns as well as the way he integrated them all into the fundamental stance of his monastic vocation—an understanding and sense of monasticism that is fuller than that of most monks. The many homey details found in the letters express the human dimension of his monastic living. Merton was a good letter writer. There is a warmth of friendship that is very beautiful. Many friends are mentioned by name. The closings are oftentimes very touching.

So let me close with one of Merton's:

I appreciate the loyalty of so many old friends and the interest of the new ones. I shall continue to feel bound to all of you in the silence of prayer. Our real journey in life is interior: it is a matter of growth, deepening, and of an ever greater surrender to the creative action of love and grace in our hearts. Never was it more necessary for us to respond to that action. I pray that we may all do so. God bless you. With all affection in Christ.

Thomas Merton

Note: These letters have now been published in *The Road to Joy,* pp. 92-121.

Father Louis' First Book:
The Spirit of Simplicity

It could be questioned whether Merton can be properly called the "author" of *The Spirit of Simplicity*. A large part of the book is translation and part of it is compilation. Nonetheless, it is the compilation and commentary of Father Louis that turns a significant Chapter report into an even more significant volume of formative theology.[1]

Although Thomas Merton's name never appears in the volume, it opens with a six-page foreword by this "Cistercian Monk of Our Lady of Gethsemani." Then there is Merton's translation of the report of the 1925 General Chapter of the Order of Cistercians of the Stricter Observance: "The Spirit of Simplicity: Characteristic of the Cistercian Order." There is inserted within the text of the report eleven plates of twelfth-century Cistercian monasteries and the "Plan of a Typical Cistercian Abbey of the Twelfth Century." Part Two begins on page 76 and is entitled: "Saint Bernard on Interior Simplicity." In the course of the following sixty pages Merton presents a number of texts of Saint Bernard concerning simplicity in a fuller theological sense and amply comments on them. He closes his volume with a three-page "Conclusion."

---

1. It could also be argued whether this is properly speaking Merton's "first book." His work on Jean-Marie Chautard's *The Soul of the Apostolate* was quite simply a work of translation as far as Merton was concerned. The twenty-eight-page *Thirty Poems* can hardly be considered a book.

The Foreword

After seeking to dispel some of the more superficial and popular understandings of the concept of simplicity, Merton notes that "entering into the fundamentals of our Rule, our usages, our ascetic practices, our traditions, and the teachings of our Fathers we find that the deeper we go the deeper and more significant concept of simplicity do we obtain: and this concept is always more and more intimately bound up with the very essence of Cistercian spirituality." Because the report itself "deals principally with external simplicity," Merton "considered it worthwhile" to add a second part on the teaching of Saint Bernard in regard to interior simplicity. This is typical of Merton. He wants to get to the heart of the matter, to the inner vitalizing core that gives life to the externals, calls them forth, and justifies their existence.

Merton identifies the mind of Saint Bernard with that of the Cistercian founders as it is expressed in the *Little Exordium* and sums it up this way: *"Getting rid of everything that did not help the monk to arrive at union with God by the shortest possible way."*[2] For Merton this meant not just getting rid of sin and "all the pleasures, vanities and useless occupations of the world," but even *"the discarding of means of getting to God that were less direct."*[3] Merton sees a good witness to this in the architecture of the twelfth-century Cistercians. Thus he includes in his volume some pictures of the better remaining examples. Still, Merton notes that his definition "leaves out one most important point, which is the fact that all this takes place because the intellect and the will of the monk seek one object alone, God as He is in Himself, not merely as reflected in His creatures or in His gifts."[4]

---

2. *The Spirit of Simplicity*, p. iii. Italics in all quotations are Merton's.

3. *Ibid.*, pp. iii-iv.

4. *Ibid.*, pp. iv-v.

Merton dedicated this little volume "to the memory of a great Cistercian, one of the saints and mystical theologians of the Golden Age, Blessed William of St. Thierry, on the eighth-hundredth anniversary of his death (September 8, 1948)." In closing his foreword, Merton brings forth a quotation from William's *Golden Epistle*, which gives two definitions of simplicity: "Simplicity may be defined as a *constant and unchanging desire for one object and Him alone* . . . simplicity is the perfect conversion of the will to God, asking one thing of God, and desiring that alone."[5]

Part One: The Spirit of Simplicity

The first part of the volume is made up of the Chapter document. This, of course, was not written by Merton, only translated. However, he does add a number of footnotes. These sometimes explain terms which might be unfamiliar to the general reader. Sometimes they explain how monks observed certain points at the time Merton worked on this text. (In some instances practices have changed considerably since the forties when Merton wrote this.) At times Merton indicates some later studies on the matter at hand. A few times he makes his own comment, usually in favor of good taste. The notes give evidence to a certain amount of naïveté on the part of the young monk. I have little doubt that a more mature Merton would have at least been tempted to make more comments on the text. The document as it stands serves as a basis for the more positive theological contribution Merton makes in the second part of the book.

The report is composed of a brief introduction and five sections. The short first section speaks of "Interior Simplicity." Exterior simplicity has to find its true source in interior sim-

---

5. *Ibid.,* pp. v-vi.

plicity, which the document sums up in Saint Benedict's fundamental phrase, "*vere Deum quaerit* [he truly seeks God]."[6]
The document sees this tied in with the act of contemplation
in a way that might surprise some today: "Grace will make
every monk, who does not stop somewhere along the road in
his quest for God, a *contemplative*. . . . Contemplation: that is to
say, a *simple* gazing upon God, a gaze that is fused with love,
and which is the prelude to that *consummation in unity* and,
therefore, perfect simplicity which is the beatific vision."[7] The
monk seeks to be free for this contemplation; he "works to
remove every obstacle that stands in the way of his progress
in union with God."[8] One of the direct consequences of this is
exterior simplicity.

Section two, which is also quite short, is an appeal to the
monks: "Let Us Be True to the Ideal of Our Founders." It leads
into the next section which forms the bulk of the report.
"Simplicity in the *Little Exordium*" explores at length the pro-
visions or institutes of this early document as a witness to the
aims of the founders of Cîteaux. This reflects the purpose of
the report: "All the General Chapter requires is that we make
use of the *Little Exordium* and other material of St. Bernard's
time in order to show in a few pages, calculated to be of service
to the monasteries of our Order, what great importance our
first Fathers attached to the *Spirit of Simplicity*."[9] The aim of
this third section was to show that "a jealous love of simplicity
sums up the reasons why Cîteaux was founded."[10] The *Little
Exordium* has little to say about architecture as such, so the
document appeals to Saint Bernard, especially to his *Apologia*,
as well as to the appraisals of some modern scholars and
architects. This material occasions Merton's inclusion of the

---

6. Saint Benedict, *RB1980. The Rule of Saint Benedict*, chapt. 58.
7. *The Spirit of Simplicity*, pp. 6-7.
8. *Ibid.*, p. 10.
9. *Ibid.*, p. 22.
10. *Ibid.*, p. 51.

photographs of a number of twelfth-century Cistercian monasteries.

The fourth section, "Anxiety of the General Chapters to Preserve the Spirit of Simplicity," traces their activity through the Golden Age (1098-1256) and the Silver Age (the next hundred years) to the period of decline. The frequency of Chapters greatly decreased while Christendom struggled with the Black Death, incessant wars, the appointment of unsuitable hierarchs, and the beginnings of Protestantism. "But the chief thing was that the Order was less and less prepared to defend itself against these external enemies and against the general environment of a Christianity that was worse than tepid. This helplessness was due, in large part, to the loss of the spirit of simplicity."[11]

The hortatory concluding chapter picks up the story with the establishment of the Order of Cistercians of the Stricter Observance in 1892 as a result of the activity of Pope Leo XIII. The report sees the establishment of what at the time was called the Order of Reformed Cistercians as a moment of renewal, which sent the newly formed Order to its ancient sources: the Cistercian Fathers, Saint Benedict, and back to the monastic fathers of the East: Climacus, Chrysostom, Basil, and others. The emphasis again is on interior simplicity. And thus the report concludes with the then latest word from the papal throne. In the year just prior to the writing of this report, Pope Pius XI approved the revised constitutions of the Order, and in his Brief, *Monachorum vita,* he gave his own expression of the simplicity characteristic of the Cistercians: "Their purpose in this is to devote themselves exclusively to contemplation: *ut ad caelestia unice intenderent animus.*"[12]

This report, attributed to the 1925 General Chapter, certainly lacks the logical order that might give it more strength.

---

11. *Ibid.,* p. 60.
12. *Ibid.,* p. 74.

It reveals a certain naïveté and lack of historical criticism. But it would be wrong to fault something that was written in 1925 and commented on by a young monk in 1948 because it did not incorporate the insights we have as a result of the many excellent studies that have been made in more recent years. There is a certain polemic in the text, albeit clothed in a pastoral alb. The many texts from the Fathers make it a fruitful document for *lectio*. It presents a valid thesis and challenge. It challenged Merton. Let us explore his response.

Part Two: Saint Bernard on Interior Simplicity

In this second part, which he calls an appendix to the report, Merton does not use any of the texts of Saint Bernard which were quoted in the report itself. His choices show how wide his familiarity was with the writings of the saint. He chooses what he considers to be a "few extremely important quotations" from Saint Bernard's writing, mostly his classic work on the *Song of Songs*, along with supporting texts from such lesser known sources as the *Sermons for Easter* and *Sermons for the Feast of Saint Michael and the Angels*, which do more than just throw light on what is in the report. Rather, as Merton sees it, they "give us the massive dogmatic foundation upon which the Cistercian doctrine of simplicity is built as upon granite."[13] Unlike the report, then, which narrows down its considerations in part to the more specific tradition of the Stricter Observance, Merton's articulation of some of the foundational teaching of Saint Bernard is applicable to and can be fruitful for all Cistercians and, indeed, for all Christians.

Before setting forth his chosen texts and commenting on them, Merton offers in his brief introductory section a very concise presentation of what he considers "the key to the

---

13. *Ibid.*, p. 76.

whole mystical theology of St. Bernard." We were first made in the image and likeness of God. We were made not the very image of God as is the Son, but to the image of God, dependently participating in the divinity. When we sought in our primogenitor to be like God in our own right, we lost, not the indelible image of God that is of our very nature, but our likeness to him, our rectitude. The tragedy, our unhappiness, lies in this: The image within us, which consists in simplicity, immortality and freedom of will, is constantly confronted with the disfigurement of our duplicity and our servitude to sin and death.

The whole aim of the Cistercian life is to set us apart from the world with its doings and ambitions, so that we may be purified and brought to perfect union with God by recovering our lost likeness to him. The many exercises and observances of the life are to make us keenly aware of our miserable state of division and lead us to prayer and to open ourselves to the mercy of God. As we are healed by his grace and freed from our unlikeness and all the fear that goes with it, confidence and love grow, the image is more and more fully restored. Merton concludes: "Saint Bernard does not hesitate to promise, as the *normal term* of the Cistercian life of simplicity, a perfect union of wills with God by love, which he calls the Mystical Marriage."[14]

In the following pages Merton sets forth four basic texts. But he divides his treatment into five sections.

The first section, "Man's Original Simplicity," uses *Sermons 81 and 82 on the Song of Songs.* It is a concise presentation of Saint Bernard's anthropology, much of which Merton already set forth in his introduction to Part Two. The human person is made in the resemblance of God but is not equal to God. For God, to be (*esse*) is to live happily (*beatum vivere*)—the highest and most pure simplicity. The second is like unto this: For the

---

14. *Ibid.*, p. 80.

human to be (*esse*) is to live (*vivere*). And this makes it possible for the human to ascend, by God's grace, to participate in the divine *beatum vivere*.

In the Fall, this simplicity of the human soul remains truly unimpaired in its essence. It is only covered over by duplicity, deceit, simulation and hypocrisy. The resulting contradiction between our essential simplicity and the duplicity engendered by sin confront each other, causing confusion and pain. Desire for the earthy, rather than the immortal, makes us like that which we desire: darksome and unstable. We have put on the mortality of sin and death.

What we desire to possess, we fear to lose. This fear has "discolored" our liberty, covered it over and concealed it. Our liberty is held in the bonds of our fear. If we desired nothing—simply loved God whom we possess—we would fear nothing, we would be filled with confidence and remain free, strong and beautiful.

Everything has been "reduplicated": our simplicity by duplicity, our immortality by the death of sin and of the body, our freedom by the desire of material concerns, our likeness to God by unlikeness. Our essential goodness has been defiled, but not destroyed, by accidentals, making us not only unlike God but unlike our true selves. We have become like the beasts. Merton notes here how in this Saint Bernard vindicates the goodness of human nature. The first step in our ascent to God is to know ourselves, and the labor of our lives is to be our true selves, returning to the simplicity, immortality and freedom that belong to us. "The whole of Cistercian simplicity can be summed up in this," says Merton. He goes on to develop the steps: First we come to know the truth about ourselves—sincerity; then we accept it—meekness, self-effacement, humility; then we rid ourselves of all that is useless—mortification of the lower appetites through external simplicity, of the internal sense and intellect through devotion, study, and methods of prayer, and of the will (which is most important) through obedience. The document of the Chapter has spoken at length about the first means of mortification, so Merton goes on in the following sections to bring forth Saint Bernard's teaching on the latter two.

Merton's second section, on "Intellectual Simplicity," uses primarily *Sermons 35* and *36 on the Song of Songs,* but also *31, 37* and *38,* along with references to the fourth of the *Sermons on Various Subjects* and the treatises on *The Steps of Humility and Pride, On Consideration,* and *On the Love of God.*

We are capable of a twofold ignorance: of ourselves and of God. It we truly know ourselves, we will be humble and fear God; this is the beginning of wisdom and the opposite of pride. If we know God, we will be filled with love and hope, possess him and come to the perfection of wisdom. Knowing ourselves without this knowledge of God could lead us to despair. Intellectual simplicity allows us to be taught by God's love. Contemplation is the "extreme simplicity of an intuition," beyond all concepts, images and pictures, phantasms and discursive acts of the mind. There is no figure; there is the direct contact of love, the created effect of love. The fact that intellectual simplicity is brought to its fullness through the unity brought about by love, leads naturally to the next section: "The Simplification of the Will."

In the third of his *Sermons for the Feast of the Resurrection,* Saint Bernard notes that there is a twofold leprosy that can infect the human heart: attachment to one's own will and attachment to one's own judgment. In the light of this, Merton divides his third section into two parts to consider each of these.

There can be and should be a good self-love which seeks one's own perfection according to the will of God. The self-will that is leprous is the intention to please self, "intention" here understood as the actual movement of the will toward the object of its selfish desires. This self-will is destroyed by obedience that is subordinated to charity and integrated with the communal life. Such obedience seeks *nihil plus, nihil minus, nihil aliter quam imperatum,* nothing more, nothing less, nothing other than what is commanded by the superiors, the Rule, and the brethren. It abandons all internal argument. Our will becomes one with the common will.

Attachment to our own judgment is more pernicious. The more strongly we are so attached, the more we are deceived, setting up our own standard and unable to see our self-deception. We are freed from this by following the example of Christ, who submitted himself to Mary and Joseph, who submitted his human will, however good it be, to the will of his Father. For Saint Bernard, the will is the highest faculty; hence unity of wills in charity produces the highest and most perfect simplicity. It is the work of the Holy Spirit, and it will be realized perfectly only in heaven.

Suddenly Merton becomes universal and eschatological: "Indeed the whole work of achieving this final magnificent and universal simplicity of all men made one in Christ will be His eventual triumph at the last day."[15] And he goes on to say with emphasis: *"Hence we see that the very essence of Cistercian simplicity is the practice of charity and loving obedience and mutual patience and forbearance in the community life which should be on earth an image of the simplicity of heaven.* We begin to see something of the depth of this beautiful Cistercian ideal!"[16]

Merton goes on to develop a line of thought here that is perhaps key to his own future development. I shall quote the entire paragraph, because it sums up much of what he has been saying all along but also opens up this new vista:

> Cistercian simplicity, then, begins in humility and self-distrust, and climbs through obedience to the perfection

---

15. *Ibid.,* p. 126. Merton, writing almost half a century ago, does not hesitate to use the masculine form in a generic sense. I am sure if he lived today he would be most sensitive to the issues involved in this.

16. *Ibid.*

of fraternal charity to produce that unity and peace by which the Holy and Undivided Trinity is reflected not only in the individual soul but in the community, in the Order, in the Church of God. Once a certain degree of perfection in this social simplicity is arrived at on earth, God is pleased to bend down and raise up the individuals who most further this unity by their humility and love to a closer and far more intimate union with Him by mystical prayer, mystical union.[17]

From the time he first consciously set out on the spiritual journey, Merton was always keenly interested in the mystical dimension of the Christian life, keenly desirous of mystical prayer, mystical union with God. In this little book he will go on to teach that such union is the expected outcome of following the Cistercian way of simplicity. Here Merton shares a certain insight. He perceives that the ones on whom God bestows such grace are those individuals who most further social simplicity, most further unity and peace. Perhaps we have here the key as to why Merton began to be very sensitive to social issues and was as actively involved in the peace movement and in the questions of racial integration as his contemplative vocation and the demands of his vows would allow. A deep and sincere loving concern for peace and unity would dispose him to receive the mystical graces of union for which he so longed. Merton goes on here to say (summing up his whole next section in so doing):

The culmination of Cistercian simplicity is the mystical marriage of the soul with God, which is nothing else but the perfect union of our will with God's will, made possible by the complete purification of all the duplicity of error and sin. This purification is the work of love and

---

17. *Ibid.*, pp. 126-27.

particularly of the love of God in our neighbor. Hence it is inseparable from that social simplicity which consists in living out the *voluntas communis* [the common will of the community] in actual practice.[18]

Sanctified by participation in the common will, which is God himself working in us and in the Church, the individual is prepared for the graces of infused contemplation.

As we have already stated, the fifth section, "Perfect Simplicity, Unity of Spirit with God," was essentially summed up by Merton in the quotation above. To develop his teaching more concretely, Merton brings forth a text from Saint Bernard's treatise *On the Love of God* concerning the fourth degree of love. First we love ourselves for our own satisfaction. Then we begin to love God because we perceive how good he is to us. As we become more and more aware of his goodness, we begin to love him in himself. Finally, we come to be so one with God in love, that we love even ourselves only because he loves us. This complete unity of will with God is the consummation of simplicity.

It may seem a bit paradoxical that we attain a more perfect simplicity when we are more fully absorbed in this union. But the essence of the human soul is to be like God. We are most truly ourselves when we are identified with him, when we lose our own will and are one will, one spirit with him. We come to forget ourselves, all our own wishes and desires, and come to have only the wishes and desires of God. "This, then, is the ultimate limit of Cistercian simplicity: the simplicity of God Himself, belonging to the soul, purified of all admixture of self-love, admitted to a participation in the Divine Nature, and becoming one Spirit with the God of infinite love."[19]

---

18. *Ibid.*, p. 127.
19. *Ibid.*, p. 135.

Conclusion

Merton's conclusion is brief. He begins by noting that when a person has been sanctified and has come to be closely united to God, there is a certain beauty about him or her. The soul communicates even to the flesh which it informs something of its own peace and supernatural radiance. The whole bearing of the person is so marked. So, too, the inner simplicity of Cistercian communities gave expression to the expansive, simple beauty we see in their buildings and (a great literator like Merton would note this) in their writings. If these things are the natural expression of an interior simplicity, it is also true that their simplicity can in turn foster interior simplicity. Hence the exhortations of the General Chapter, to which Merton joins his voice in practical ways, to foster simplicity in our lives and in our buildings. Merton urges his readers to turn to the literature of the early Cistercians. We can never hope to acquire the spirit of simplicity characteristic of our Order if we never enter into contact, directly or at least indirectly, with the sources from which it flowed.[20] Nevertheless, he notes that study is not enough. We need to practice all that Saint Bernard has set forth and to devote ourselves to fervent prayer to the Holy Spirit.

This little book, quietly published on the eve of Merton's monumental best-selling autobiography, ended his career as an obedient translator. I do not think the new demand for his writings was the only reason why Merton moved on in his literary career. When he undertook this third volume in The Cistercian Library Series, Merton moved beyond mere translation to begin to share something of the rich spiritual insight he himself had attained through his contact with the "sources." He had found in Saint Bernard an anthropology

---

20. *Ibid.*, p. 138.

that imperiously demanded that one be all that one can be, and a solid dogmatic foundation on which to build an integrated spiritual theology that can be universal, immanent, and eschatological. He was ready for the great literary vocation that lay ahead of him.

Thomas Merton and His Own
Cistercian Tradition

In the last pages of *The Secular Journal,* Thomas Merton sums up his spiritual journey toward the Church and monastery:

> From Gilson's *Spirit of Medieval Philosophy* I learned a healthy respect for Catholicism. Then *Ends and Means* taught me to respect mysticism. Maritain's *Art and Scholasticism* was another important influence, and Blake's poetry. Perhaps also Evelyn Underhill's *Mysticism,* though I read precious little of it. I was fascinated by the Jesuit sermons in Joyce's *A Portrait of the Artist as a Young Man!* What horrified him, began to appeal to me. It seemed to me quite sane. Finally G. F. Lahey's *Life of Gerard Manley Hopkins;* I was reading about Hopkins' conversion when I dropped the book and ran out of the house to look for Father Ford.[1]

It is not surprising that this author would be influenced primarily by authors and their books.

In the preface to *A Thomas Merton Reader,* published in 1962, six years before his tragic death, Merton summed up his monastic years:

> I would say that my life at Gethsemani has fallen roughly into four periods. First, the novitiate. I was a novice in 1942-1944. Those were hard years, before the days when radiators were much in favor during the winter, when

---

1. *The Secular Journal of Thomas Merton,* pp. 268-69.

the hours of communal prayer were much longer, when the fasts were much stricter. It was a period of training, and a happy, austere one, during which I wrote little. The best Gethsemani poems belong to this period.

At the end of the novitiate my health broke down, and I was appointed to write and do translations of French books and articles. I was also studying philosophy and theology in preparation for ordination to the priesthood. This second period extends from 1944, my first vows, to ordination in 1949. At first, the writing was very bad. . . . In 1946 I wrote *Seven Storey Mountain*, in 1947 *Seeds of Contemplation*, and in 1948 *The Waters of Siloe*. After ordination, in 1949, there was another brief period of poor health and nervous exhaustion. I was almost incapable of writing for at least a year and a half after I became a priest. Then after a rest period in the hospital, I wrote *The Ascent to Truth* and *Bread in the Wilderness* (both about 1951) and finished *The Sign of Jonas*, 1952. In 1951 I was appointed the Master of Scholastics, that is, of the young monks studying for ordination in the monastery. This entailed a fair amount of work preparing conferences and classes. Books like *The Living Bread* and particularly *No Man Is an Island* and *The Silent Life* belong to the end of this period.

Finally, a fourth stage. In 1955 I was made Master of the Choir Novices. This is an office involving considerable work and responsibility. No writing of any account was done in 1956, but after that it was possible to produce short books or collections of essays, and some poetry. *Disputed Questions*, *The Wisdom of the Desert*, *The Behavior of Titans*, and *New Seeds of Contemplation* belong to this last period. So too do more recent essays on nuclear war, on Chinese thought, on liturgy, and on solitude.[2]

---

2. *A Thomas Merton Reader*, pp. viii-ix.

It is notable that in all of this literary remenacing, Merton does not mention specifically any Cistercian Father or any of the work he did concerning them. Prior to entering the monastery, he does not seem to have had any contact with the Cistercian tradition. But once he entered the Cistercian life, he so immersed himself in it that it became the very matrix of his life and thinking. In his early days, as he was assimilating Cistercian spirituality, Merton wrote about the Cistercian Fathers explicitly. When he served the community as master of scholastics and as novice master he spoke about them constantly; his notes and his taped conferences are full of them. Later they cropped up spontaneously in his writings, the paradigm against which he evaluated what he was then absorbing. One of his favorites, Adam of Perseigne, would find his place in the final talk Merton gave a few hours before his sudden death.[3]

When Merton first entered the monastery, there was, as he said in the epilogue of *The Spirit of Simplicity*, little of the Cistercian Fathers available in English. But this did not hinder him. He not only found no problem in reading the Latin texts in the Migne collection, he strongly believed that translations always lacked something of the original Latin text.[4] He studied these texts very carefully. This is witnessed by his frequent use of quotations from them in his early writings and his talks to scholastics and novices, as well as by the underlining and annotations found in the volumes of the Fathers which he used.

Bernard of Clairvaux

One of Thomas Merton's earliest assignments was to translate a report from the Cistercian General Chapter, entitled *The*

---

3. *The Asian Journal of Thomas Merton,* p. 333.
4. *A Thomas Merton Reader,* p. 317.

Spirit of Simplicity and provide a suitable introduction for it. He not only did what he was asked to do but also gathered a complementary selection of texts from Saint Bernard on interior simplicity in its fullness. He translated these and commented on them, turning the report into a full book.[5]

This second part of *The Spirit of Simplicity* has been published in a volume in the Cistercian Studies Series with two other early Bernardine essays of Merton.[6] He wrote a five-part study of Bernard and John of the Cross for *Collectanea Cisterciensia,* which expresses his concern of the period when he was writing *The Ascent to Truth.* In these essays we can detect a certain struggle Merton experienced in trying to respond both to the rich, fully human, patristic heritage Bernard offered him and the exciting, stimulating, scholastic approach which John of the Cross was able to integrate with a high mystical theology. Bernard's approach would be the one to win him over. In the prologue to *The Sign of Jonas* he will write:

> I found in writing *The Ascent to Truth* that technical language, though it is universal and certain and accepted by theologians, does not reach the average man and does not convey what is more personal and most vital in religious experience. Since my focus is not upon dogmas as such, but only on their repercussions in the life of a soul in which they begin to find concrete realization, I may be pardoned for using my own words to talk about my own soul.[7]

The third piece in the Cistercian Studies volume witnesses to another early concern of Merton—the superiority of the contemplative life. In an extensive essay, which was first published serially in *Collectanea Cisterciensia* and later appeared as

5. See chapter above, "Father Louis' First Book: *The Spirit of Simplicity.*"

6. *Thomas Merton on Saint Bernard,* pp. 103-57.

7. *The Sign of Jonas,* pp. 8-9.

Marthe, Marie, et Lazare in French, Merton is at pains to establish that the apostolic life, though it may have a fullness beyond the purely contemplative life, as Bernard acknowledges, has true value only insofar as it flows out of contemplation. And thus the contemplative life is in itself more important or of greater dignity. Merton's argumentation here is not all that easy to follow, nor that cogent. Later he himself would comment negatively about such preoccupation.[8]

The eighth centenary of Bernard's death led to a spate of publishing on the saint. Merton translated the Papal Encyclical produced for the occasion. He wrote an introduction to it, and it was published as *The Last of the Fathers*. He was invited to introduce other works. His preface to *Bernard de Clairvaux*, a collection of studies published by the Historical Commission of his Order, shows the increasing influence of Bernard on Merton.[9] The piece is filled with scriptural texts and allusions. We might say it is a very Bernardine piece about Bernard. In line with his earlier concentration, Merton sees that Bernard added to the Cistercian reform "an emphatic call to contemplative union with God."[10] At the same time Merton begins to reveal a more integral understanding of Bernard as a "man of his times . . . a many-sided saint."[11] This is further evidenced in the next piece.

His introduction to Bruno Scott James' *St. Bernard of Clair-*

---

8. In the preface to *A Thomas Merton Reader* he would write: "It would be a still greater misapprehension to say I am simply trying to prove that the contemplative life is 'better than the active life. . . .' Not only am I not trying to prove these propositions, but stated in this bald and unqualified manner, I do not even hold them. It is true that fifteen years ago I was able to get excited about such theses, but I have come to see that controversy about speculative matters of this sort is not only a waste of time but is seriously misleading. We are all too prone to believe in our own programs and to follow the echo of our own slogans into a realm of illusion and unreality" (p. viii).

9. See "St. Bernard, Monk and Apostle" in *Disputed Questions,* pp. 260-76.

10. *Ibid.,* p. 263.

11. *Ibid.,* p. 262.

vaux Seen through His Selected Letters he considered important.
At his behest it was included in *A Thomas Merton Reader* in the
section on "Mentors and Doctrines."[12] It revealed Thomas
Merton's growth in his appreciation for Bernard in line with
his own personal growth. Merton had had his experience on
the corner of Maple and Fourth and now beheld all with a
greater integrity. He had a new appreciation for Bernard the
man. He appreciated the letters because they so well brought
out the human dimension of this great saint:

> They [the letters] show the man as he is, and because he
> is so much a man, readers who forget that saints must
> be men may sometimes be inclined to question his
> saintliness. . . . Bernard is sent to instruct us how human
> a saint must be to forge out the will of God in the heat
> of the affairs of men. . . . He had the humility to be
> himself in the thick of a silly argument. He had the good
> grace to admit that a saint might possibly have to bicker
> with another saint . . . the angry Bernard, the passionate
> Bernard . . . the merciful Bernard, the gentle long-suffer-
> ing monk who could be as tender as a mother.[13]

As Merton noted in his brief literary biography quoted above,
liturgy came more to the fore in a later period of his life. In
Seasons of Celebration he published one of his most beautiful
pieces on Saint Bernard: "The Sacrament of Advent in the
Spirituality of Saint Bernard."[14]

It is undoubtedly Saint Bernard, the "Theologian of the
Cistercian Life" (as Merton's friend Jean Leclercq would name
him), who received the most attention from Merton. But besides Bernard's prominence as the master of the Cistercian
school, there would be the influence of Gilson. As we have

---

12. *A Thomas Merton Reader*, pp. 315-19.

13. *Ibid.*, pp. 316-17.

14. *Seasons of Celebration*, pp. 61-87.

seen above, Gilson was one of the first to open the way for Merton toward Catholicism. Merton's respect for him never diminished, and Gilson's masterful work, *The Mystical Theology of Saint Bernard* was most carefully studied and wholly accepted by Merton.[15] But Merton read all the significant Cistercian Fathers and spoke and wrote on them as occasion offered.

Aelred of Rievaulx

Special attention received the "Bernard of the North," Bernard's disciple Aelred, the abbot of Rievaulx. Merton has an extensive piece on him, which looks like it was on the way to becoming a book.[16] It is an important piece and I shall return to it later in this chapter.

As one of his first projects for Cistercian Publications, Merton wrote an introduction for Fr. Amedee Hallier's *Monastic Theology of Aelred of Rievaulx.* Here again we see the later Merton rejecting earlier attitudes:

> Let us be quite clear the monastic theology of Aelred is not a partisan "theology of monasticism." It is not an apologia for the life of the monk, and not a kind of gnostic system organized to prove some supposed superiority of "the contemplative life," urging a flight to ineffable convulsions.[17]

He saw that "the Christian life is, for Aelred, simply the full flowering of freedom and consent in the perfection of friend-

---

15. There is a copy of Gilson's work in the Merton Center at Columbia University with Merton's underlining and marginalia, which indicate the care with which he studied this book.

16. This has been edited and published serially in *Cistercian Studies,* 20 (1985): 212-23; 21 (1986): 30-42; 22 (1987): 55-75; 23 (1988): 45-62; 24 (1989): 50-68.

17. Amedee Hallier, *The Monastic Theology of Aelred of Rievaulx,* p. viii.

ship. Friendship with other human beings as an epiphany of friendship with God." Merton notes that "not so long ago, some of Aelred's books were kept under lock and key in Trappist libraries."[18]

William of Saint Thierry

Merton never wrote a particular essay on Bernard's closest friend, William of Saint Thierry, but he considered him "a profound and original theologian and a contemplative in his own right."[19] He dedicated *The Spirit of Simplicity* to him, "one of the saints and mystical theologians of the Golden Age" and quoted him extensively in the foreword.

Guerric of Igny

With regard to the fourth of the evangelists of Gîteaux, Guerric of Igny, we have the opportunity to get a sampling of Merton's more ordinary treatment of the Cistercian Fathers in his talks to the juniors at Gethsemani. The transcription of two taped talks have been published in *Cistercian Studies* in 1972.[20] For Merton, "Guerric was really deep and very spiritual and very mystical."[21] And as Merton opens him up for his novices, he is also very much alive, very practical and down to earth. It is in these intimate talks that we best see how the Cistercian Fathers reverberated in the mind and heart of this twentieth-century Cistercian Father.

There is a more formal treatment of Guerric of Igny and his liturgical sermons in Merton's introduction to the translation of Guerric's Christmas sermons.

---

18. *Ibid.*, pp. xi-xii.

19. Manuscript on "Saint Aelred of Rievaulx," p. 20.

20. Thomas Merton, "Guerric of Igny's Easter Sermons" in *Cistercian Studies*, 7 (1972): 85-95.

21. *Ibid.*, p. 85.

Other Cistercian Fathers

Other Cistercian Fathers turn up in Merton's published writings. There are poems about Saint Alberic[22] and Saint Malachy.[23] When *Cistercian Studies* began publishing Sr. Penelope's translation of the sermons of Isaac of Stella, Merton provided an introduction for this "not the least interesting of the Cistercian writers."[24] He found him a "more independent thinker and less subject to the dominant influence of Bernard,"[25] whose writings reminded him "at times of Eckhart in their tone."[26] Merton's spirit resonated with this abbot, who withdrew from a large and important Cistercian abbey to an *eremus*, a poor and lonely island foundation.

Merton provided an introduction for another Cistercian Father, Adam of Perseigne, one of his favorites.[27] Earlier he had written about Adam's theory of monastic formation in an essay that was published in Charles Dumont's French translation.[28] Adam was for Merton something of a mentor in his duties as novice master. His admiration for the Abbot of Perseigne remained until the end. In his final talk at Bangkok he brings him forth to illustrate a basic monastic theory.[29] When the earlier essay was further developed, Merton gave it a new title, one that witnessed to his own development: "The Feast of Freedom." Adam, Aelred, as well as all the other great Cistercian Fathers led Merton into the same direction.

But Merton didn't have an unbounded admiration for all

---

22. *Selected Poems of Thomas Merton*, pp. 44-45.
23. *Ibid.*, pp. 75ff. This poem is reproduced in *A Thomas Merton Reader*, pp. 177-78.
24. Louis Merton, "Isaac of Stella: An Introduction to Selections from His Sermons" in *Cistercian Studies*, 2 (1967): 243.
25. *Ibid.*.
26. *Ibid.*, p. 244.
27. "The Feast of Freedom: Monastic Formation according to Adam of Perseigne" in *The Letters of Adam of Perseigne*, vol. 1, pp. 3-48.
28. "La formation monastique selon Adam de Perseigne" in *Collectanea Ordinis Cisterciensium Reformatorum*, 19 (1957): 1-17.
29. *The Asian Journal of Thomas Merton*, p. 333.

the twelfth-century Cistercian writers. An example of this is Garnier of Langres:

> Garnier was not deep and not spiritual and not mystical. He was a literal-minded person with a lot of learning. As a matter of fact he is quite interesting. On the liturgy, he has a lot of little statements about what they did at the time and what they thought they were doing and why they did it. But these are just little statements of historical fact. Today Garnier would be a scientific-minded critic. But a scientific-minded critic in the Middle Ages is just about zero, because he has nothing to work on. . . . He's finished, he's dated, he's way back. He is no more modern than a twelfth-century concept of the universe.[30]

He goes so far as to say: "His Work . . . is not in English at all, and if it ever gets translated into English that won't be too soon."[31] This does, though, give us another indication as to the extent to which Merton worked his way through the pages of Migne[32] and explored all the published writings of the early Cistercian Fathers.

Above I have mentioned the monograph that Merton was working on, entitled "Saint Aelred of Rievaulx." This is a significant piece of work. In placing Aelred in context, Merton gives a fine synopsis of Cistercian history and especially literary history from the foundation in 1098 up until the death of Becket (+1170). But I think one of the valuable elements of this work is the insight that Merton has as a later Cistercian writer into these early Cistercian writers. Indeed, as I read the pertinent section I ask myself if this is not a candid insight into Merton himself as a Cistercian writer:

---

30. "Guerric of Igny's Easter Sermons," pp. 85-86.
31. *Ibid.*
32. He read Garnier in Patrologia Latina, vol. 205.

The rich and elegant vitality of Cistercian prose—most of which is sheer poetry—betrays an overflow of literary productivity which did not even need to strive for its effects: It achieved them, as it were, spontaneously. It seemed to be second nature to St. Bernard, William of Saint Thierry, Adam of Perseigne, Guerric of Igny, to write with consummate beauty prose full of sound and color and charm. There were two natural explanations for this. The first is that the prolific Cistercian writers of the Golden Age were men who had already been thoroughly steeped in the secular literary movements of the time before they entered the cloister. All of them had rich experience of the current of humanism that flowered through the twelfth-century renaissance.

There is a second explanation for the richness and exuberance of theological prose in twelfth-century monasteries of Cîteaux. If contact with classical humanism had stimulated a certain intellectual vitality in these clerics, it also generated a conflict in their souls. The refined natural excitements produced by philosophical speculation, by art, poetry, music, by the companionship of restless sensitive and intellectual friends merely unsettled their souls. Far from finding peace and satisfaction in all these things, they found war. The only answer to the problem was to make a clean break with everything that stimulated this spiritual uneasiness, to withdraw from the centers in which it was fomented, and get away somewhere, discover some point of vantage from which they could see the whole difficulty in its proper perspective. This vantage point, of course, was not only the cloister, since Ovid and Tully[33] had

---

33. Ovid (43 BC-18 AD) was a classical Latin poet known for his erotic verse and manuals for lovers. Tully is a classical nickname for Marcus Tullius Cicero (106-43 BC), an outstanding orator and writer responsible for bringing Greek philosophical thinking to the Western world.

already become firmly established there, but the desert—the *terra invia et inaquosa* [the land without path or water], in which the Cistercian labored and suffered and prayed. . . .

The tension generated by the conflict between secular humanism and the Christian humanism, which seeks the fulfillment of human nature through ascetic renunciation and mystical union with God, was one of the proximate causes of the powerful mystical writing of the Cistercians.

However, once these two natural factors have been considered, we must recognize other and far more decisive influences, belonging to a higher order. . . . It is the relish and savor that only experience can give, that communicates to the writings of the twelfth-century Cistercians all the vitality and vividness and impassioned sincerity which are peculiarly their own. . . . The White Monks speak with accents of a more personal and more lyrical conviction that everywhere betrays the influence of an intimate and mystical experience. . . . It is the personal, experiential character of Cistercian mysticism that gives the prose of the White Monks its vivid freshness. . . .

Since the theology of the Cistercians was so intimately personal and experiential, their exposition of it was bound to take a psychological direction. All that they wrote was directed by their keen awareness of the presence and action of God in their souls. This was their all absorbing interest.[34]

Many scholars have noted that Merton's writings show a rather superficial knowledge of the Eastern religions. But when I traveled in the East and spoke with the spiritual

---

34. Manuscript on "Saint Aelred of Rievaulx," pp. 10-17.

masters there who had come into contact with Merton on his last journey, they said they had never met anyone from the West who had so fully understood their ways. I think that the same might be said of Merton and the Cistercian Fathers. Certainly many scholars know more about the Fathers and the early history of the Cistercian Order. But few, if any, so fully understand their spirit as does this twentieth-century Cistercian Father. Moreover, no one has been able to express so fully and clearly what these Fathers have to say for our times and for the renewal of the Cistercian Order. We cannot but profit from choosing Thomas Merton for our *lectio*, from spending time with him and letting him lead us into a deeper, fuller understanding and appreciation of the Cistercian Fathers.

Like Father Like Son:
Bernard of Clairvaux and Thomas Merton

In 1990 we celebrated the nine-hundredth anniversary of the birth of Bernard of Clairvaux. Today there is no one of his sons as famous as Thomas Merton. There are many remarkable similarities between these two great men, some more significant than others. First, both were born in France; Bernard at Fontaines-les-Dijon in 1090 and Merton at Prades on January 31, 1915. Perhaps more important than is readily realized in the life of each is the fact that they both lost their mothers at an early age.

Both went to excess in their early adulthood, in both directions. Merton's excesses are fully reported in his autobiography, *The Seven Storey Mountain*, and successive biographies.[1] Once they entered on the monastic way, both gave themselves to monastic fasts and labor without regard for their relatively weak constitutions. But virtue lies in the middle. Both had to learn, and, before they did, they both managed to do lasting harm to their physical constitution and had to live with the consequences.

Merton came to the cloister a little later than Bernard (Bernard was twenty-three when he arrived at the gates of Cîteaux; Merton arrived at Gethsemani at the age of twenty-six), but both wholeheartedly embraced the monastic life and remained true to it until death in spite of many temptations, if

---

1. Michael Mott's *The Seven Mountains of Thomas Merton* is the biography authorized by the Merton Legacy Trust in accord with the will of Thomas Merton. See also my own complementary study, *Thomas Merton, Brother Monk: The Quest of True Freedom*.

this is what we want to call them. Bernard spurned more than one miter, while Merton steadily declined appeals to come out from the cloister to assume an active leadership role in the causes he championed. Merton did entertain the possibility of a move within the monastic way, with the hope of finding greater solitude, and Bernard often bemoaned that he was not able to enjoy more fully the peace and solitude of his cloister.

There is no doubt, Bernard and Louis were both men of exceptional genius and well-developed literary talent. Even during their own lifetimes their richly poetic prose was well known, much in demand, and had significant impact on the Church and society. A much more restricted and Christianized society was more affected by the earlier writer. But the later monk reached an extraordinarily large and varied audience, not only within the most powerful nation and linguistic group on earth, but also within many other sectors of human society by virtue of the many published translations of his writings.

Both were moved powerfully by grace to seek the fullness of the mystical life. Both wrote extensively on this search for God. Both saw it as the proper goal of every Christian life and, through published writings and personal letters (both were exceptionally good letter writers[2]), sought to encourage the pursuit of it. Their earlier writings were almost exclusively in this vein, along with more specifically monastic themes. The final work of each was decidedly contemplative in its orientation, yet more widely embracing: Bernard's *De consideratione* and Merton's *Climate of Monastic Prayer.* Yet, long before they reached these final syntheses, circumstances and the love of Christ urged them to expand their contemplative conscious-

---

2. We have a good collection of Bernard's letters, which he himself began to compile for us, in *Sancti Bernardi Opera*, vols. 7 and 8. The most complete English translation is the collection of Bruno Scott James, *The Letters of Saint Bernard of Clairvaux*. Merton's letters have been edited and published in five volumes; see the bibliography.

ness to embrace a wounded humanity with its many pressing needs. While the younger Merton who wrote the triumphalistic piety of *The Seven Storey Mountain* might have embraced a crusade, we can hardly conceive of his doing this in the last years of his life. Yet he remained, as did Bernard, a man of his times. Some today wish to edit his non-inclusive language and the attitudes it sometimes betrays, rightly judging, I believe, that if he were alive today he would wish to do that himself.

Both, much to the regret of many and to our perduring loss, died at a relatively young age. Bernard died in 1153 at the age of sixty-three; Merton died in 1968, when he was only fifty-three years old. How much more they could have given us!

The New Man

While many of the similarities between the two may seem merely coincidental, there is no doubt that Bernard, the "Theologian of the Cistercian Order," did exert an important formative influence on his spiritual son. Abbot Flavian Burns relates how, when Professor Dan Walsh first read Merton's *The New Man,* he exclaimed: "*The New Man*—the new Merton!" Walsh was not wholly accurate here. In what is Merton's most definitive theological work, he brought forth much of what he had learned from his father, Bernard, earlier in his life. Merton readily acknowledged this.[3] Yet he did not merely repeat the teaching of the abbot of Clairvaux. He gave it new, powerful expression in the existential terminology of our times. And perhaps he even dared to press it a bit further than did the earlier writer. In any case, Merton set forth the imaging of Christ in our creation and recreation in a way that did not betray Bernard. Rather it challenges us more powerfully in its contemporary expression.

---

3. "Without going into great detail, let us sketch out some of the broad outlines of the picture freely, following the thought of Saint Bernard" (*The New Man,* p. 104).

In the foundational chapter of *The New Man*, "Image and Likeness," and elsewhere in the book Merton was dependent on the same Bernardine passages he had excerpted in the second part of *The Spirit of Simplicity*. We are made to the very image and likeness of God. Unlike the rest of creation, for us to be is to be alive. Our simplicity is not as complete as that of God, for whom to be is to be alive happily. Our whole being seeks happiness, but it can and has eluded us. Instead of being true to who we are, we have taken on a certain duplicity. In our ignorance we have not known our true selves. Nor have we truly known God. For, if we did, we would know we are of God and that the goodness of God is such that all is ours as gift. Rather, like Prometheus we seek to steal, or at least try to earn in some way, from God the happiness for which we long. Instead of embracing wholly the divine will in the truth of our being, becoming one in mind and in heart with God and thus with our true self, we seek rather to create a false self. We, who are wholly of God insofar as we are, seek to be something of ourselves. Thus we are alienated not only from ourselves but also from God. We will not find our true selves looking at ourselves. We will find our true selves only in God and in union with him in love. This is love knowledge, something beyond anything the rational intellect can attain, for we are made in the very image and likeness of God, partakers of the divine nature and life. When we love ourselves and others as God loves us, then we have come to our true selves. "To love like this is to become a god."[4]

Merton is so filled with the spirit of Bernard and the men of Bernard's time, that like Bernard he reaches for a mythological figure to help bring out the fullness of the biblical teaching. He sets forth a "Promethean theology"[5] using Hesiod's sad

---

4. These are the last words of Saint Bernard that Merton quotes in *The Spirit of Simplicity*, p. 135.

5. The title of the second chapter in *The New Man*, pp. 21-48.

figure to image our psychological situation of guilt, rebellion, frustration, insecurity, and self-alienation.

The breakthrough that Bernard made in image theology for his times in his treatise *On Grace and Free Choice* and in his *Sermons on the Songs of Songs,* Thomas Merton made for our times, if we would but hear him. Like Bernard, Merton grounds a powerful spiritual teaching on profound theological insights. A clear grasp of these insights can give us a strong impulse to live an exciting, Christ-centered and Christ-empowered life, the life Saint Paul was speaking about and living. This is not the place to develop the full thesis of *The New Man,* but the modern existential thinker who wants *lectio* that is fully in the spirit of Saint Bernard yet benefits from the subsequent development in human thought and Christian doctrine can find no better place to do it than in Thomas Merton and, most especially, in his *The New Man.*

Bernard wrote habitually out of his own lived experience. There were few exceptions to this. Merton learned early in his monastic literary career that abstract writing, with an impersonal and sort of scientific approach, did not work for him.[6] His efforts in writing *The Ascent to Truth* brought on his only, though somewhat perduring experience of writer's block. Though the nervous breakdown he experienced during this same period was not brought on solely by this. He was still struggling with the integration of himself as a writer and a monk. Merton saw something of this same struggle in Bernard and other early Cistercian Fathers whom he so greatly admired.

Doctor Mellifluus

In 1953, on the occasion of the eighth centenary of Saint Bernard's death, Pope Pius XII issued an encyclical honoring

---

6. See *The Sign of Jonas,* pp. 8-9.

the "Last of the Fathers": *Doctor Mellifluus*. Merton published an English translation of the encyclical with an extensive introduction. As we read what he writes about the Mellifluous Doctor we cannot help but think that much of what he is saying fits the author himself. "It seems," he writes, "that one of the things Saint Bernard wanted to get away from when he entered Cîteaux was literary ambition." But, Merton writes, "all sanctity is born of conflict."[7] He contrasts the rich natural endowments of Bernard and the stark monastic simplicity that the saint sought, and goes on: "Saint Bernard seems to have thought it possible to renounce everything of the first element in his soul and live entirely by the second."[8] Besides highlighting this conflict that was so much of an element in Merton's own early monastic life, Merton also points to Bernard's widespread influence, noting that

> one of the signs of a spiritual revival that is really spiritual is that it affects every kind of life and activity around it, inspires new kinds of art, awakens a new poetry and a new music, even makes lovers speak to one another in a new language and think about one another with a new kind of respect.[9]

The romantic in Merton perhaps goes a bit far here. Nonetheless, it is true that both Bernard and Merton affected life around them in many ways, inspired poetry and music, and challenged us to have greater respect for ourselves and for each other.

---

7. *Thomas Merton on Saint Bernard*, p. 47 and 26.
8. *Ibid.*, p. 25.
9. *The Last of the Fathers*, p. 29.

Thomas Merton and Byzantine Spirituality

Thomas Merton has without doubt been the most influential Catholic writer on the American scene in the twentieth century. His heart was indeed ecumenical. It stretched beyond the bounds of ecumenism in the strict sense to embrace all that is good in the human spirit, even if that be found among so-called pagans or Marxists. I don't think it is possible to exaggerate the importance of the influence of Byzantine spirituality, and especially that of the Fathers of Eastern Christendom, on the development of Merton's well-integrated spirituality. We might say that Merton's Christian life, writings and spirit are marked from their first serious awakening to their end by the influence of the Christian East.

When he went to Rome in 1933, still very much a hedonist, it was the great Byzantine mosaics that called him forth and changed the tourist into a pilgrim. In *The Seven Storey Mountain* he tells us:

> I was fascinated by these Byzantine mosaics. I began to haunt the churches where they were to be found. . . . And now for the first time in my life I began to find out something of who this Person was that men called Christ. It was obscure, but it was a true knowledge of Him, in some sense, truer than I knew and truer than I would admit. . . . And now I think for the first time in my whole life I really began to pray—praying not with my lips and with my intellect and my imagination, but

praying out of the very roots of my life and of my being,
and praying to the God I had never known.[1]

At the end of his journey, in the last book which he prepared
for publication, *The Climate of Monastic Prayer*, Merton opens
with the desert tradition and goes on to share the kernel of the
teaching of the *Philokalia*, the classical collection of Byzantine
spirituality. As we progress through the text, which offers a
clear and relatively concise history of contemplative spirituality and the teachings of the masters, we come upon such
names as Isaac of Niniveh, Saint Ammonas, Evagrius Ponticus, Saint Basil, Saint Gregory of Nyssa, the Pseudo-
Dionysius, Saint Nilus, and others from the Byzantine
tradition.

His First Contacts

The influence of the great writers of the Eastern Church first
came to Merton mediated through the Cistercian writers
whom he read extensively in his early years in the monastery.[2]
As his studies moved forward, he came, in part with the help
of Gilson, to recognize and identify these sources.[3] But it was
the desert tradition, whose delightful, pithy, and profound
sayings so attracted him, that opened Merton to pursue the
evolution of this strong, rich current of spirituality. In his very
interesting and informative series of taped talks, *Solitude and
Community: The Paradox of Life and Prayer*, Keith Egan said of
Merton: "He began to read the literature that came out of the
desert, the Christian desert of the fourth century. And one of
the most important books he wrote is his shortest, and that is
The Wisdom of the Desert . . . . The study that lies behind the

---

1. *The Seven Storey Mountain*, pp. 108-11.
2. John Eudes Bamberger, O.C.S.O., "Thomas Merton and the Christian East"
   in Pennington, ed., *One Yet Two: Monastic Tradition East and West*, p. 443.
3. Etienne Gilson, *The Mystical Theology of Saint Bernard*.

writing of this little book was transforming and changed Merton's life forever."[4]

When in 1960 he published this short collection of sayings, Merton wrote a very rich introduction of twenty-two pages. In it he traced the spiritual path laid out by the Fathers. It begins with a "clean break," called compunction, a lament over the madness of our attachments to unreal values. Through solitude and labor, poverty and fasting, charity and prayer, the old superficial self is purged away and the true secret self is permitted to emerge. The monk moves toward purity of heart:

> . . . a clean, unobstructed vision of the true state of affairs, an intuitive grasp of one's own inner reality as anchored or rather lost in God through Christ. This leads to *quies*, the sanity and praise of a being that no longer has to look at itself, because it is carried away by the perfection of being that is in it. And carried where? Wherever Love itself, or the Divine Spirit, sees fit to go. Rest, then, was a kind of simple no-whereness and no-mindedness that had lost all preoccupation with a false or limited "self."[5]

The terminology Merton uses here is not that of the desert tradition. By this time the Fathers had opened Merton to other even broader influences, but first they opened him to their own immediate heirs.[6] Merton went on to expand and deepen his vision through the developing theology of the Christian East: the Cappadocians, especially Gregory of Nyssa, Eva-

---

4. Keith Egan, *Solitude and Community: The Paradox of Life and Prayer*, tape 3, "The Desert: Place of Discovery."

5. *The Wisdom of the Desert*, p. 8.

6. Merton goes on to say: "In many respects, therefore, these Desert Fathers had much in common with Indian Yogis and with Zen Buddhist monks of China and Japan" (*ibid.*, p. 9).

grius Ponticus, who really belongs to the desert tradition and, above all, Maximus the Confessor.

In his first full-length work on spirituality, a study of the teaching of John of the Cross entitled *The Ascent to Truth,* Merton devotes many pages in the first and third chapters to those "great theologians of darkness: Saint Gregory of Nyssa and Pseudo-Dionysius."[7] The former he hails as "the most important and the most neglected of the early Christian mystical theologians, the Father of Christian apophatic mysticism."[8] He depends here largely on Gregory's scriptural commentaries of Ecclesiastes, Psalms and the Song of Songs. He traces out Gregory's journey from light to darkness with the Mosaic imagery of the burning bush, the pillar of cloud and finally the darkness of Sinai, and suggests a parallel with the three dark nights of John of the Cross. On page 27 he speaks of *theoria physike*, distinguishing the positive and negative aspects of it. But I do not think that at this time this important element of Eastern Christian spiritual teaching had the impact on him that later was to be, in my opinion, very significant. In the introduction to *The Sign of Jonas*, Merton himself clearly indicated the shortcomings of the very dry intellectual approach to this teaching which he presented in the *The Ascent to Truth*.[9]

A Fundamental Insight

Some years later Merton had the opportunity to study the Greeks more fully and reflect more profoundly on them, as he prepared and gave a course to his fellow monk-priests on Christian mysticism. We only have the notes of these lectures, but they are quite full and, while they lack his usual rich literary style, they do have his candid clarity and forceful

---

7. *The Ascent to Truth,* p. 25.

8. *Ibid.,* p. 319.

9. *The Sign of Jonas,* p. 9.

impact.[10] It is here that he highlights the central place of Gregory of Nyssa more in detail, indicating his influence on the Cistercian writers. He also notes Nyssa's influence on the Syrians through Saint Macarius, and on the Greeks in general through Maximus the Confessor.[11] In the same notes he studies extensively and deeply the meaning of the "spiritual senses," disagreeing with the interpretations or understanding of previous Western writers such as Poulain and Olphe Gaillard. Merton adopts a more integrated view, seeing the "spiritual senses" closely allied with the bodily senses that have been freed and purified by mortification, virginity and passive purification, and elevated and spiritualized by grace and the operation of the Holy Spirit until they approach a full restoration of that state of paradise where God was enjoyed by the senses "deifying the body" (Saint Gregory Palamas).[12]

More important is the insight he attains into *theoria physike* under the tutelage of Evagrius Ponticus, whom he strongly defends, and Maximus the Confessor. The spiritual life is seen to involve three stages: 1) *bios praktikos (praxis)*, the purification of the body, of the senses, of the passions, leading to *apatheia*, the *puritas cordis* of John Cassian, something more than detachment, a positive openness to reality, to the divine; 2) *theoria physike*, a spiritualized knowledge of the created, a sort of natural contemplation, which does reach on to the divine *oikonomia*, God's plan for things, and the *logoi* of things, the divine plan within things. At its higher levels it reaches to the contemplation of the spiritual; 3) *theologia*, the contemplation of the Trinity without form or image.

I believe it was the understanding of *theoria physike* that enabled the zealous, ascetic, world-despising young monk,

---

10. *An Introduction to Christian Mysticism—From the Apostolic Fathers to the Council of Trent.* A manuscript of lectures given at the Abbey of Gethsemani. At the end of the foreword we find the date: Vigil of the Assumption, 1961.

11. *Ibid.*, p. 31.

12. *Ibid.*, pp. 35-42.

who constantly fought with his own human gifts for poetry and literature, to reintegrate his natural appreciation and love for the wonders of creation and all that the good God made and to go on to become the very full and integrated person he became. Merton himself said: "We can in fact say that the lack of *theoria physike* is one of the things that accounts for the stunting of spiritual growth among our monks today."[13]

He goes on to say: "It is by *theoria* that man helps Christ to redeem the *logoi* of things and restore them to Himself. . . . This *theoria* is inseparable from love and from a truly spiritual conduct of life. Man must not only see the inner meaning of things but he must regulate his entire life and his use of time and of created beings according to the mysterious norms hidden in things by the Creator, or rather uttered by the Creator himself in the bosom of His Creation."[14] I would like to quote more extensively from Merton here, because this matter is absolutely central to the understanding of his spiritual development and outlook:

Man by *theoria* is able to unite the hidden wisdom of God in things with the hidden light of wisdom in himself. The meeting and marriage of these two brings about a *resplendent clarity* within man himself, and this clarity is the presence of divine Wisdom fully recognized and active in him. Thus man becomes a mirror of the divine glory and is resplendent with divine truth not only in his *mind* but in his *life*. He is filled with the light of wisdom which shines forth in him, and thus God is glorified in him. At the same time he exercises a spiritualizing influence in the world by the work of his hands which is in accord with the *creative wisdom of God* in things and in him.

13. *Ibid.*, p. 56.
14. *Ibid.*, p. 59.

No longer are we reduced to a purely negative attitude toward the world around us, toward history, toward the judgments of God. The world is no longer seen
as purely material, hence as an obstacle to be grudgingly
put up with. It is spirit there and then. But grace has to
work with and through us to enable us to carry out this
real transformation. Things are not fully spiritual in
themselves, they have to be spiritualized by our knowledge and love in the use of them. Hence it is impossible
for one who is not purified to "transfigure" material
things. On the contrary, the *logoi* will remain hidden and
he himself will be captivated by the sensible attraction
of these things.[15]

In this last sentence I think we see the difference between these
Greek Fathers, and Merton with them, and the currently popular "creation theology." The Greeks and Merton emphasize
that it is impossible to enter into a true *theoria physike*, a true
appreciation of the creation and the presence of God in creation, without first embracing the *bios praktikos*, that purification that produces *apatheia*, a true purity of heart that enables
us to appreciate the overwhelming beauty, transfiguring the
creation without being ensnared by it. Otherwise we are in
danger of resting in the creation and becoming attached to it
and ourselves, rather than finding all in God and God in all,
being attached to him alone.

Also, the Greeks and Merton never stop at the *theoria
physike*, the wonders of the creation, even transfigured by God,
but are ever conscious of this as a stage on the way to true
theologia, to finding our true place within the very life of the
Trinity, we who have been made truly and mysteriously one
with the Son in baptism, we who have been "deified." In this

---

15. *Ibid.*

context, and in this context alone, does *theoria physike* or "creation theology" attain its full meaning, as does human life.

As has been said, Merton's "discovery" and full perception of *theoria physike* had a profound formative and liberating influence on him. Later in this chapter I will return to further indications of this. Let us now continue to look at the influences of the Eastern Christian spiritual heritage on Merton and his writings.

At the same time as Merton was preparing and teaching this course he was preparing one of his own significant and weighty theological volumes, *The New Man*. In this study he depends heavily on Western theologians: Augustine and Bernard, Aquinas and Ruysbroec. But the names of Eastern Fathers keep cropping up: Clement of Alexandria and Gregory of Nyssa, Cyril of Jerusalem and others. The influence is perhaps more profoundly marked by the extraordinary frequency with which he employs Greek words in this text. We find *pneuma, pneumatikos, metanoia, antitypos* and *parousia* all used more than once. More significant is the very extensive study of *parrhesia*, which Merton well defines as "free spiritual communication of being with Being."[16]

During this same period Merton also wrote a rather poor piece on Mount Athos, "the last important Christian survival of the typical ancient monastic colonies."[17] I don't think Merton can be blamed for the poverty and inaccuracies of this piece. He never had the opportunity to visit the Holy Mountain (something I am sure he would have loved to have done) and had to depend on the accounts of others of which he noted: "In such books one rarely receives any insight into the profound religious mystery of Athos."[18] He was enthusiastic about the idea of Athos, and proposed a similar Western monastic repub-

---

16. *The New Man.*, p. 76.
17. "Mount Athos" in *Disputed Questions*, p. 70.
18. *Ibid.*, p. 69.

lic with a similar freedom of monastic expression. He was a bit pessimistic about the future of the Holy Mountain. No doubt he would be elated at its present vigorous revival, even to the inclusion of more monks from Holy Russia.[19]

In the same volume in which he published the Athos piece, Merton added a study on "The Spirituality of Sinai," largely a commentary on Saint John Climacus' *Ladder*.[20] The piece is rather rough, filled with slang (fanatical windbag, busting him in the teeth, Climacus was nuts, etc.) and homey details (such as his reaction to the reading of the *Ladder* in the community refectory at Gethsemani). The piece was occasioned by the publication of Archimandrite Lazarus Moore's translation, which Merton praises. He appreciates more the stream of spirituality that Climacus represents than this "tough, hard-hitting, merciless book,"[21] for "all Russian literature and spirituality is tinged with the ferocity and paradox of Sinai."[22] From Sinai, too, the practice of the Jesus Prayer came to Athos and to Russia: "Let the rememberance of Jesus be present with each breath, and then you will know the value of solitude," says Climacus.[23]

Merton and the Ever-Holy Russia

Russia had a special place in the heart of Merton. The only Athonite monk that he seemed to get close to as a living reality was the humble and saintly procurator of the Russian monastery of Saint Panteleimon, Father Siloan. Through the writings of Father Siloan's disciple, Father Sophrony, Merton was able to appreciate this simple and profoundly prayerful man, who never lost his love for solitude even in the midst of serving a

---

19. For a detailed description of this renewal of Athos see my book, *O Holy Mountain*.
20. *Disputed Questions*, pp. 83-93.
21. *Ibid.*, p. 84.
22. *Ibid.*, p. 88.
23. *Ibid.*, p. 93.

monastery of hundreds of monks.[24] In his preface to Sergius Bolshakoff's *Russian Mystics*, Merton gives evidence of an extensive knowledge of Russian monastic history. Saint Nilus, in his controversy with institutional monasticism represented by Saint Joseph Volokolamsk, was of special interest, especially since much of Evagrius' teaching has come down to us under Saint Nilus' patronage. But for Merton, Saint Seraphim of Sarov was "without doubt the greatest mystic of the Russian Church."[25] In him there is a balance between the ascetic tradition and austerity (*poddvig*), repentance and tears and a humanism filled with joy, open to life, gentle, and profoundly compassionate. He has "evangelical and patristic purity, pure and traditional theology, ingenuous amazement of the divine light shining through the darkness."[26] Saint Seraphim's is a mysticism of light (albeit based on the apophaticism of Pseudy-Dionysius and Maximus) which approaches the Invisible as visible in creation *transfigured* in divine light.

Merton's interest in the Russian writers in time ranged far beyond the monastic and even the religious, properly so-called. In the late 1950s he even made an abortive attempt at learning Russian so that he could read them in their original language. *Conjectures of a Guilty Bystander* is sprinkled with names like Belinsky, Lenin and Berdyaev, along with pages devoted to Evdokimov.[27] His next published journal includes a quote from Yelchaninov in the prelude.[28]

This broadening is indicated in a curious way in an interesting piece that reflects Merton's first days in his hermitage. He had never gotten very far from the desert tradition. In those

24. *Conjectures of a Guilty Bystander*, p. 147. Merton refers to Father Siloan as "Staretz Sylvan"; this is undoubtedly a slip of memory.

25. *Russian Mystics*, p. xii.

26. *Ibid.*, p. xiii.

27. *Conjectures of a Guilty Bystander*, pp. 308-10. Merton gives the title "Father" to Evdokimov, perhaps mistakenly thinking that this lay theologian is a priest.

28. *Woods, Shore, Desert*, p. 3.

days he wrote a very fine piece on "The Spiritual Father in the Desert Tradition."[29] Dom John Eudes Bamberger rightly notes that the ideal of the spiritual father had become a part of his own identity.[30] Merton also wrote a piece on the cell, drawing from the same source.[31] But the biographical piece that opens *Raids on the Unspeakable* is the piece to which I am referring. In "Rain and the Rhinoceros" Merton tells us of sitting in his hermitage on the hill above the Abbey, reading by his Coleman lantern (he did not yet have electricity there).[32] On this particular rainy night he was reading Philoxenos (a sixth-century Syrian), seeking to understand better the solitude to which he was so drawn. On this night he read Philoxenos' ninth *memra* (on poverty) to dwellers in solitude. Merton heard again that "there is no explanation and no justification for the solitary life, since it is without a law."[33] "Leave the rule of the world where he [Christ] has left the law, and go out with him to fight the power of error."[34] Merton concludes his passage on Philoxenos saying: "Today the insights of a Philoxenos are to be sought less in the tracts of theologians than in the meditations of the existentialists and in the Theater of the Absurd."[35]

Merton's favorite among the modern Russian writers seems to be Boris Pasternak. He wrote three articles on this poet and novelist[36] whom he saw as "immensely more important than Sholokov."[37] He finds Pasternak's witness to be "essentially Christian."[38] The Christianity Pasternak presented is "reduced to the barest and most elemental essentials: intense awareness

---

29. *Contemplation in a World of Action*, pp. 269-93.
30. Bamberger in Pennington, ed., *One Yet Two: Monastic Tradition East and West*, p. 449.
31. *Contemplation in a World of Action*, pp. 252-59.
32. *Raids on the Unspeakable*, pp. 9-26.
33. *Ibid.*, p. 14.
34. *Ibid.*, p. 19.
35. *Ibid.*
36. "The Pasternak Affair" in *Disputed Questions*, pp. 3-67.
37. *Ibid.*, p. 13.
38. *Ibid.*, p. 12.

of all cosmic and human reality as 'life in Christ,' and the consequent plunge into love as the only dynamic and creative force which really honors this 'life' by creating itself anew in Life's—Christ's—image."[39] Merton sensed a very deep oneness with Pasternak and expresses it powerfully and beautifully in the first letter he addressed to the Russian, some months prior to the explosion over the Nobel Prize:

> I feel much more kinship with you, in your writing, than I do with most of the great modern writers in the West. That is to say that I feel that I can share your experience more deeply and with greater intimacy and sureness. . . . With other writers I can share ideas, but you seem to communicate something deeper. It is as if we meet on a deeper level of life on which individuals are not separate beings. In a language familiar to me as a Catholic monk, it is as if we were known to one another in God.[40]

He could write thus because by this time Merton had fully integrated the outlook and experience of *theoria physike*, and Pasternak comes out of the same living tradition; they experience the creation in the same basic way and express this in their poetry and writing. Merton actually points to this in his first article on Pasternak:

> Pasternak, whether he knows it or not, is plunged fully into midstream of the lost tradition of "natural contemplation"[41] which flowed among the Greek Fathers after it had been set in motion by Origen. Of course the Tradition has not been altogether lost, and Pasternak has come upon it in the Orthodox Church. The fact is

---

39. *Ibid.*
40. *Six Letters*, pp. 3-4.
41. Merton's English expression for *theoria physike*, as we have seen above.

clear in any case: he reads the Scriptures with the avidity and the spiritual imagination of Origen, and he looks on the world with the illuminated eyes of the Cappadocian Fathers.[42]

Merton appreciated this "sophianic" view of the cosmos as a creation impregnated by *hagia sophia*, holy wisdom, the word and love of God in other Russian writers such as Solovév and Berdiaev (Merton's articles on Pasternak bring out his extensive familiarity with the Russian authors), but he identified most strongly with Pasternak's spirit so akin to his own. This is perhaps why he shared with him in his second letter a secret he had shared with only three others: his dream about the Jewish girl Proverb.[43]

It portrays a very intimate and, I think, a very important insight into why that well-known experience on the streets in Louisville had such an impact on him. Not only was it impacted with the rich imagery of a dream but with the ever-deepening insight into *theoria psysike* that Merton was integrating into his perception of reality. Merton was in many ways a very private person, even in his many published journals. We owe to the extraordinary openness of this most unusual friendship this beautiful and touching revelation that throws so much light on the integration of its writer.

Merton's Last Days

In the last journal that Merton himself prepared for publication, the one flowing from his two-week trip to the west coast and New Mexico in May of 1968, Merton is still with his Russian friends. He returns to Theophane the Recluse with his salutary advice for prayer of the heart: "Not to run from one

---

42. *Disputed Questions,* p. 17.
43. See chapter above, "Growing in Compassion," pp. 27-28.

thought to the next . . . but to give each one time to settle in the heart. *Attention:* Concentration of the spirit in the heart. *Vigilance:* Concentration of the will in the heart. *Sobriety:* Concentration of the feeling in the heart."[44]

Here too, in his constant quest for true freedom, Merton writes: "I wonder about the definition of Orthodoxy as hostility to rules."[45] He is reflecting on a quote from Yelchaninov: "Orthodoxy is the principle of absolute freedom."[46]

The most important thing about this journal, especially as it has been published with inclusion of some of the photographs that Merton took on the journey, is that it is a magnificent witness to the full flowering of *theoria physike* in its author. It conveys his cosmic and earthy contemplation in the way it can best be conveyed: through poetics and artistry. This severe critic of technology (and in his criticisms I think he was right on the mark) does not hesitate with the true freedom of the son of God to use a bit of technology—the camera—to produce some real art that powerfully highlights and shares his contemplative insight.

The Asian Journal, his last, published posthumously, does not mention any Russians or Eastern Christian Fathers. This may be due to the editors. In his notes for the talk he gave at the Spiritual Summit Conference of the Temple of Understanding in Calcutta he indicated his intention to speak on the Hesychast tradition, Mount Athos, and Orthodox monasteries.[47] In actual fact Merton did not employ these notes and rather spoke extemporaneously.

In those same notes Merton speaks about the qualities needed for true dialogue between the different traditions: "It must be reserved for those who have entered with full seriousness into their own monastic tradition and are in authentic

44. *Woods, Shore, Desert,* p. 16.

45. *Ibid.,* p. 20.

46. *Ibid.,* p. 3.

47. *The Asian Journal of Thomas Merton,* p. 311.

contact with the past of their own religious community—besides being open to the tradition and to the heritage of experience belonging to other communities."[48] Speaking of such a person in another article published after his death, he adds:

He is fully "Catholic" in the best sense of the word. He has a unified vision and experience of the one truth shining out in all its various manifestations, some clearer than others, some more definite and certain than others. He does not set these partial views up in opposition to each other but unifies them in a dialectic or insight of complementarity. With this view of life he is able to bring perspective, liberty and spontaneity into the lives of others. The finally integrated man is a peacemaker.[49]

Merton certainly was this kind of man. He entered very deeply into and lived deeply his own tradition. He also entered deeply into the traditions of others. In his introductory essay to *The Wisdom of the Desert*, Merton says: "Love demands a complete inner transformation—for without this we cannot possibly come to identify ourselves with our brother. We have to become, in some sense, the person we love."[50] Merton did this. He loved and he identified. Finally, in *Conjectures of a Guilty Bystander* he says: "I am more convinced that my job is to clarify something of the tradition that lives in me and in which I live: the tradition of wisdom and spirituality that is found not only in Western Christendom but in Orthodoxy."[51] As Rowan Williams said in his comparative study of Evdokimov and Merton: "Merton's spirituality . . . would not be what it is without his devoted and careful study of Greek patristic

---

48. *Ibid.*, p. 316.
49. *Contemplation in a World of Action*, p. 212.
50. *Wisdom of the Desert*, p. 18.
51. *Conjectures of a Guilty Bystander*, p. 176.

thought and the Desert Fathers" and, I would add, all that flowed out of them.[52] And not only study, but an assimilation and integration that produced a profound and profoundly beautiful lived synthesis.

52. Pennington, ed., *One Yet Two: Monastic Tradition East and West*, pp. 452-53.

Thomas Merton and Centering Prayer

Speaking about centering prayer Thomas Merton would say:

> The fact is, however, that if you descend into the depths of your own spirit . . . and arrive somewhere near the center of what you are, you are confronted with the inescapable truth, at the very root of your existence, you are in constant and immediate and inescapable contact with the infinite power of God.[1]

And on another occasion:

> *. . . a man cannot enter into the deepest center of himself and pass through the center into God unless he is able to pass entirely out of himself and empty himself and give himself to other people in the purity of selfless love.*[2]

In my first book on centering prayer, *Daily We Touch Him,* I offered a number of texts from the writings of Merton on this kind of prayer. But nowhere in the writings he published have we found a really personal expression of his own use of the prayer. Merton was a very private person. Although he published an autobiography and a number of personal journals, these were all carefully edited. However, in his letters Merton was sometimes quite open, especially with spiritual persons who he felt were aligned with him, even though they were of

---

1. *The Contemplative Life,* p. 28.

2. *New Seeds of Contemplation,* p. 64. Throughout this chapter, all italics in Merton quotes are his.

114

very different traditions. It is in a letter to a Sufi scholar, Aziz Ch. Abdul, that Merton gives a rather long and clear description of his ordinary way of praying:

> Now you ask about my method of meditation. Strictly speaking I have a very simple way of prayer. It is centered entirely on attention to the presence of God and to His will and His love. That is to say that it is centered on *faith* by which alone we can know the presence of God. One might say this gives my meditation the character described by the prophet as "being before God as if you saw Him." Yet it does not mean imagining anything or conceiving a precise image of God, for to my mind this would be a kind of idolatry. On the contrary, it is a matter of adoring Him as invisible and infinitely beyond our comprehension, and realizing Him as all. My prayer tends very much to what you call *fana*. There is in my heart this great thirst to recognize totally the nothingness of all that is not God. My prayer is then a kind of praise rising up out of the center of Nothingness and Silence. If I am still present "myself" this I recognize as an obstacle. If He wills He can then make the Nothingness into a total clarity. If He does not will, then the Nothingness actually seems itself to be an object and remains an obstacle. Such is my ordinary way of prayer, or meditation. It is not "thinking about" anything, but a direct seeking of the Face of the Invisible. Which cannot be found unless we become lost in Him who is Invisible.[3]

This is quite simply centering prayer.

The idea of God as being at the center was brought home to Merton early in his life, in an experiential rather than concep-

---

3. *The Hidden Ground of Love*, pp. 63-64.

tual way—in a way that spoke to him daily, almost constantly, in one of the most formative periods of his life. When he was ten years old, his father took him to live in St. Antonin. This was a medieval shrine town in the Midi that still preserved much of its medieval character when the Mertons moved there in 1925. As a shrine, the church stood prominently at the middle of the town. All streets led to it, or away from it, depending on one's perspective. The impression was unmistakable that the church and the One who dwelt therein were at the center of things. Twenty years later Merton recorded this impression, which daily impinged on the young adolescent:

> . . . the center of it all was the church. . . . Here, in this amazing, ancient town, the very pattern of the place, of the houses and streets and of nature itself, the cliffs and trees, all focused my attention upon the one, important central fact of the church and what it contained. Here, everywhere I went, I was forced by the disposition of everything around me, to be always at least virtually conscious of the church. Every street pointed more or less inward to the center of the town, to the church. Every view of the town, from the exterior hills, centered upon the long grey building with its high spire.[4]

In his writings, Merton speaks of the sad effects of not living out of the center, out of the Reality that is:

> We are so obsessed with *doing* that we have no time and no imagination left for *being*. As a result, men are valued not for what they are but for what they *do* or what they *have*—for their usefulness. When man is reduced to his function he is placed in a servile, alienated condition.

---

4. *The Seven Storey Mountain*, pp. 36-37.

He exists *for* someone else or even worse for some *thing* else.

Those who relinquish God as the center of their moral orbit lose all direction and by that very fact lose and betray their manhood.[5]

Presupposed to centering prayer and the first movement toward it is faith. The journey toward the center is a journey of faith, nourished by the two sources, scripture and tradition—nourished by rich *lectio*, or faith reading and sharing. In a rare instance where Merton shares one of his dreams, he speaks about this:

> I dreamt I was lost in a great city and was walking "toward the center" without quite knowing where I was going. Suddenly I came to a dead end, but on a height, looking at a great bay, an arm of the harbor. I saw a whole section of the city spread out before me on hills covered with light snow, and realized that, though I had far to go, I knew where I was: Because in this city there are two arms of the harbor and they help you to find your way, as you are always encountering them.[6]

The two arms of the harbor are, of course, scripture and tradition. With them there to guide us, we cannot get lost on our walk "toward the center." We need to turn to them daily to find our way.

The way to the center, to the experience of God, is love. From love comes our ability to sense God present. Merton goes on to speak of the first movements of this, as it might be experienced in centering prayer:

---

5. *Conjectures of a Guilty Bystander*, pp. 282 and 104.

6. *Ibid.*, p. 170.

There is a kind of pre-experiential contemplation in which the soul simply plunges into the darkness without knowing why, and tends blindly toward something it knows not. Only later is there a strong, subjective verification of the truth that this "something" toward which the soul is groping is really God Himself and not just an idea of God or a velleity for union with him.[7]

Such a plunging takes courage; it is a thing of grace. But it is only in experiencing it that we can discover that this is so:

God is grace to man, grace in such a thoroughgoing sense that it supports the whole of man's existence and can only be conceived of as grace by those who surrender their whole existence and let themselves fall into the unfathomable dizzy depth without seeking for something to hold on to.[8]

Merton gives encouraging advice to the beginner:

Be content, be content. We are the Body of Christ! We have found him because he has sought us. God has come to take up his abode in us, in sinners. There is nothing further to look for except to turn to him completely, where he is already present. Be quiet and see that he is God.[9]

If you dare to penetrate your own silence and dare to advance without fear into the solitude of your own heart, and seek the sharing of that solitude with the lonely other who seeks God through and with you, then you will truly receive the light and capacity to understand what is beyond words and beyond explanation

---

7. "The Inner Experience," *Cistercian Studies* 18:71.

8. *A Vow of Conversation*, p. 9.

9. *Conjectures of a Guilty Bystander*, p. 14.

because it is too close to be explained: it is the intimate union in the depths of your own heart, of God's spirit and your own secret inmost self, so that you and he are in truth One Spirit.[10]

A Prayer in Faith

The first "rule" or point in centering prayer is to be in faith and love to God dwelling in the depths of our being or at the center of our being.

Merton explains this movement in faith with a clear and important distinction:

If we enter into ourselves, finding our true self, and then passing "beyond" the inner "I," we sail forth into the immense darkness in which we confront the "I am" of the Almighty. . . . Our inmost "I" exists in God and God dwells in it. But it is nevertheless necessary to distinguish the experience of one's own inmost being and the awareness that God has revealed himself to us in and through our inner self. We must know that the mirror is distinct from the image reflected. The difference rests in theological *faith*. Our awareness of our inner self can at least theoretically be the fruit of a purely natural and psychological purification. Our awareness of God is a supernatural participation in the light by which he reveals himself interiorly as dwelling in our inmost self. Hence the Christian mystical experience is not only an awareness of the inner self, but also, by a supernatural intensification of faith, it is an experiential grasp of God as present within our inner self.[11]

---

10. From private notes.
11. "The Inner Experience," *Cistercian Studies* 18:9-10.

It is faith that tells us most surely that

> Christ is really present in us, more present than if he
> were standing before us visible to our bodily eyes. . . .
> By the gift of the gospel . . . we are able to see our inner
> selves not as a vacuum but as an *infinite depth*, not as
> emptiness but as fullness. This change of perspective is
> impossible as long as we are afraid of our own nothing-
> ness, as long as we are afraid of fear, afraid of poverty,
> afraid of boredom—as long as we run away from our-
> selves. . . . Hence the sacred attitude is one which does
> not recoil from our own inner emptiness, but rather
> penetrates into it with awe and reverence and with the
> awareness of mystery.[12]

This is the whole of the prayer, this moving in faith and love
to God within. Then we simply abide there, rest there in the
Reality:

> In silence, hope, expectation, and unknowing, the man
> of faith abandons himself to the divine will not as to an
> arbitrary and magic power whose decrees must be spelt
> out from cryptic ciphers but as to the stream of reality
> and of life itself. The sacred attitude is then one of deep
> and fundamental respect for the real in whatever form
> it may present itself.[13]

There is real abandonment and acceptance of whatever God
allows to happen during the time of our prayer, and yet there
is not a deadly passivity. There is a lively presence in faith and
hope:

---

12. *Ibid.* 18:211ff.
13. *Ibid.* 18:215.

What happens, happens. One accepts it, in humility, and sees it without inferring anything, or instituting any comparison with other experiences. And one walks on in the presence of God. . . . Would-be contemplatives must be on their guard against a kind of heavy, inert stupor in which the mind becomes swallowed up in itself. To remain immersed in one's own darkness is not contemplation, and no one should attempt to "stop" the functioning of his mind and remain fixed in his own nothingness. Rather we must go out in hope and faith from our own nothingness and seek liberation in God.[14]

It is faith which is at the very heart of this prayer; it is faith which guides our surrender in love, our mode of transcendence. Merton insists on this again and again:

One must let himself be guided to reality not by visible and tangible things, not by the evidence of sense or the understanding of reason, not by concepts charged with natural hope, or joy, or fear, or desire, or grief, but by "dark faith" that transcends all desire and seeks no human, earthly satisfaction, except what is willed by God and connected with his will.[15]

This act of total surrender is not simply a fantastic intellectual and mystical gamble, it is something much more serious: It is an act of love for this unseen Person, who in the very gift of love by which we surrender ourselves to his reality, also makes himself present to us. The union of our mind, spirit and life with the Word present within us is effected by the Holy Spirit.[16]

It is a contact with God in charity, yes, but also and above all in the darkness of unknowing. This follows

14. *Ibid.* 18:291ff.
15. *Ibid.* 18:13.
16. *Ibid.* 18:209.

necessarily from the fact that it goes beyond the symbols and intentions of the intellect, and attains God directly without the medium of any created image or species of the mind, but a disposition of our whole being brought about by that Love which so likens and conforms us to God that we become able to experience him mystically in and through our inmost selves as if he were our very selves. The inner self . . . now knows God not so much through the medium of an objective image as through its own divinized subjectivity.[17]

There seems to be a bit of ambivalence as Merton speaks about this experience. He sees it as something very special indeed. And it does call for a very high level of courage and fidelity. And yet it is meant for all, it is the common heritage of every child of God, every son and daughter of the Father:

Just remaining quietly in the presence of God, listening to him, being attentive to him, requires a lot of courage and know-how. This discipline of listening and of attention is a very high form of ascetic discipline, a rather difficult one to maintain. . . . In this listening, in the tranquil attention to God, God acts directly upon the one who prays, doing it by himself, communicating himself to the soul, without other means, without passing through angels, men, images or forms. . . . God and the beloved are together in great intimacy.[18]

Yet at the end of this journey of faith and love, which brings us into the depths of our own being and releases us that we may voyage beyond ourselves to God, the mystical life culminates in an experience of the presence of God that is beyond all description, and which is only

---

17. *Ibid.* 18:299.

18. *Contemplation in a World of Action,* pp. 363-64.

possible because the soul had been completely "transformed in God" so as to become, so to speak, "one spirit" with him. Yet it is nothing else but the message of Christ calling us to awaken us from sleep, to return from exile, and find our true selves within ourselves, in the inner sanctuary which is his temple and his heaven, and (at the end of the prodigal's homecoming journey) the "Father's house."[19]

It is not surprising, then, to find Merton insisting that the contemplative experience—contemplative prayer—is meant for all and not for a chosen few:

I have not only repeated the affirmation that contemplation is real, but I have insisted on its simplicity, sobriety, humility, and its integration in *normal Christian life*. This is what needs to be stressed. . . . It is surely legitimate for anyone to desire and to seek this fulfillment, this experience of reality, this entrance into truth.[20]

Necessary Dispositions

As we have seen, Merton does call for certain dispositions in order to enter into this contemplative experience, into the center. There must be a certain willingness to deny oneself at the more superficial levels and to live by faith, even a dark faith:

According to the Christian mystical tradition, one cannot find one's inner center and know God there as long as one is involved in the preoccupations and desires of the outward self. Freedom to enter the inner sanctuary

---

19. "The Inner Experience," *Cistercian Studies* 18:14-15.
20. *Ibid.* 19:145-46.

of our being is denied to those who are held back by dependence on self-gratification and sense satisfaction, whether it be a matter of pleasure-seeking, love of comfort, a proneness to anger, self-assertion, pride, vanity, greed, and all the rest. Faith . . . simultaneously a turning to God and a turning away from God's creatures—a blocking out of the visible in order to see the invisible. The two ideas are inseparable. . . . But it is important to remember that the mere blocking out of sensible things is not faith, and will not serve as a means to bring faith into existence. It is the other way around. Faith is a light of such supreme brilliance that it dazzles the mind and darkens all its vision of other realities: But in the end, when we become used to the new light, we gain a new view of all reality transfigured and elevated in the light itself.[21]

As I noted above in sharing Merton's dream, this faith needs to be nurtured by contact with the sources of scripture and tradition. It is the traditional way of *lectio, meditatio, oratio, contemplatio*—sacred reading, meditation and prayer—leading to contemplation. Merton explains this progression:

Reading becomes contemplation when, instead of reason, we abandon the sequence of the author's thoughts in order not only to follow our own thoughts (meditation) but simply *to rise above thought and penetrate into the mystery of truth which is expressed intuitively as present and actual.* We meditate with our mind, which is "part of" our being. But we contemplate with our whole being and not just with one of its parts.[22]

---

21. *Ibid.* 18:12-13.
22. *Ibid.* 18:291.

This leads to one of the obstacles we can encounter as we move into centering prayer. We need to nourish our faith, the source of our prayer, by faith reading. At the same time, however, we cannot cling to the concepts of faith that have nourished us, but must let them go in order to enter into the experience of faith through love. Faith leads us into the cloud of unknowing, and it is there, and there alone, that in this life we can immediately encounter the living God.

> In fact, the spirit sees God precisely by understanding that he is utterly invisible to it. In this sudden, deep and total acceptance of his invisibility, it casts far from it every last trace of conceptual meditation, and in so doing, rids itself of the spiritual obstacles which stand between it and God. Thoughts, natural light and spiritual images are, so to speak, veils or coverings that impede the direct, naked sensitivity by which the spirit touches the Divine Being. When the veils are removed, then I can touch, or rather be touched by, God in the mystical darkness. Intuition reaches him by one final leap beyond itself, and ecstasy by which it sacrifices itself and yields itself to his transcendent presence. In this last ecstatic act of "unknowing," the gap between our spirit as subject and God as object is finally closed, and in the embrace of mystical love we know that we and he are one.[23]

To Truly Seek God

Another possible obstacle is that we begin to seek the experience of God rather than the God of experience or the God to be experienced:

---

23. *Ibid.* 18:300.

> . . . the problem is that of taking one's subjective experience so seriously that it becomes more important than the soul, more important than God. Our spiritual experience becomes objectified, it turns into an idol. It becomes a "thing," a "reality" which we serve. We are not created for the service of any "thing," but for the service of God alone, who is not and cannot be a "thing." To serve him who is no "object" is freedom. To live for spiritual experience is slavery, and such slavery makes the contemplative life just as secular (though in a more subtle way) as the service of any other "thing," no matter how base: money, pleasures, success.[24]

When we start to seek an experience for ourselves, we are no longer seeking God, we are no longer centered on God but on self.

> If we remain in our ego, clenched upon ourselves, trying to draw down to ourselves gifts which we then incorporate in our own limited selfish life, then prayer does remain servile. Servility has its roots in self-serving. Servility, in a strange way, really consists in trying to make God serve our own needs. We have to try to say to modern man something about the fact that authentic prayer enables us to emerge from our servility into freedom in God, because it no longer strives to manipulate him by superstitious "deals."[25]

We find here a very subtle balance between seeking of self and a due expectation, since love by its very nature does want union with the Beloved. The key lies here: The seeking is really a response, the response of love, the desire that love is.

---

24. *Ibid.* 19:139.
25. *Contemplation in a World of Action,* p. 334.

One of the basic rules is that it is always a gift of God. It is always something for which we must learn how to wait. But it is also something which we must learn to *expect actively.* The secret of the contemplative life is in this *ability for active awareness,* an active and expectant awareness where the activity is a deep personal response on a level which is, so to speak, beyond the faculties of the soul.[26]

Self, then, selfishness, self-centeredness is the obstacle to centering, to being centered in God. It is the very antithesis to being to God in love, to God and therefore necessarily to others, for they are in him.

No man who ignores the rights and needs of others can hope to walk in the light of contemplation, because his way has turned aside from truth, from compassion, and therefore from God. The obstacle is in our "self," that is to say in the tenacious need to maintain our separate, external, egotistic will.[27]

The Effects of Centering Prayer

The effect of contemplation, of centering prayer, is just the opposite:

Rightly accepted, contemplative experience has its own proper effect: It increases the intensity and simplicity of a man's love for God and for his fellow men.[28]

This contemplative love leads to freedom and creativity:

---

26. *Ibid.,* p. 341.
27. *New Seeds of Contemplation,* pp. 18ff.
28. "The Inner Experience," *Cistercian Studies* 18:291.

The nothingness within us—which is at the same time the place where our freedom springs into being—is secretly filled with the presence and light of God as long as our eyes are not on ourselves and then our freedom is united with the freedom of God himself. Nothing can impede the joy and creativity of our acts of love.[29]

Contemplative insight does not only reveal to us the absorbing beauty of God and our own intrinsic beauty in him. It also reveals to us the beauty of every other person, each of whom is one with us in God. Merton speaks of his own experience here:

It was as if I suddenly saw the secret beauty of their hearts, the depths of their hearts where neither sin nor desire nor self-knowledge can reach, the core of their reality, the person each one is in God's eyes. If only they could all see themselves as they really *are*. If only we could see each other that way all the time. There would be no more war, no more hatred, no more cruelty, no more greed.[30]

In a word, the fruits of the Holy Spirit will be very present in our lives when we live out of our contemplative experience. This is surely the way we can judge the authenticity of our experience. Our contemplation should overflow into the whole of our lives, creatively bringing a certain sacredness to our environment because our eyes have been opened to the sacred that is already there, and we live and act accordingly.

All around this centered solitude radiates a universe which meditates and prays, a universe outside the uni-

---

29. *Ibid.* 19:143.

30. *Conjectures of a Guilty Bystander*, p. 142.

verse. . . . It creates a radiation, a sacred universe created by the presence of a man in this particular kind of
relation with God. And this is very important.[31]

Contemplation becomes then a constant stance. It is

spontaneous awe at the sacredness of life, of being. It is
gratitude for being. It is a vivid realization of the fact
that life and being in us proceed from an invisible,
transcendent and infinitely abundant Source . . . above
all, awareness of the reality of the Source . . . the awareness and realization, even in some sense the *experience*,
of what each Christian obscurely believes: "It is now no
longer I that live, but Christ lives in me."[32]

From these few quotes we can readily see what a rich source
we have in the writings of Thomas Merton to support our
practice of centering prayer and to understand the prayer
better. I would like to conclude this chapter with a prayer of
his:

To be here with the silence of Sonship in my heart is to
be a center in which all things converge upon you. That
is surely enough for the time being. Therefore, Father, I
beg you to keep me in this silence so that I may learn
from it the word of your peace and the word of your
mercy and the word of your gentleness to the world.
And that through me perhaps your word of peace may
make itself heard where it has not been possible for
anyone to hear it for a long time.[33]

---

31. From an unpublished journal, March 8, 1966.
32. *New Seeds of Contemplation*, pp. 1-5.
33. *Conjectures of a Guilty Bystander*, p. 161.

Thomas Merton—An Educator
for Our Times

The word "education" comes from the Latin word *educare*, which means "to lead forth." In order to lead people forth, it is necessary to go where they are and take them by the hand, as it were. It is also necessary to know where they want to go. Sometimes the person has a very clear vision as to where he or she wants to go. It is probably more often true that the one to be educated does not. It is for the educator to be in touch with the deep aspirations of the human spirit and thus to ascertain the true needs of the one who is to be led forth.

If the educator is fully in touch with humanity, he or she knows that the human mind and heart have an infinite capacity; that they are made for the Lord God, and that they can find fulfillment and rest in him alone. This knowledge is attainable to unaided human reason. The Apostle Paul assures us of this (cf. Rom 1:19-20). So does one of the greatest of Christian thinkers, Thomas Aquinas; but he also reminds us that few—very few—are ever able to attain to it in surety because of lack of time, perseverance, and mental perspicacity.[1]

Christian educators have the revelation to guide them. Through it they know that by baptism the human person, already participating in the divine being, goodness, and beauty through creation, is made an even more complete participant in divine life. The human spirit is now able to know God as he knows himself, though not in the same way in every respect, and to love God as he loves himself. In a word, he is

---

1. Thomas Aquinas, *Summa Theologiae*, I, p. 1.

able to enter into the inner life of the Trinity and to enjoy a union with the very Son of God that is beyond anything the human mind can ever fully grasp—a oneness that has its archetype in the unity of the Father and the Son within the Most Blessed Trinity: "That they may be one, Father, as I in you and you in me; that they may be one in us" (Jn 17:21). It is toward the fulfillment of these divine aspirations that the Christian educator is to lead his disciples. Whether the disciples are as yet aware of them or not, these aspirations are written into their very nature by baptism.

Thomas Merton was first and foremost a full Christian humanist, but he was also an educator. His medium was the written word. He also exercised other active and effective educational roles. For some years he was the master of the scholastics at the Abbey of Gethsemani and then for ten years the master of novices. Each of these roles required of him regular lectures or classes. When he retired from them and entered into a more eremitical life, he returned each Sunday from his hermitage in the woods and gave a lecture to his brothers in the cenobium. Happily, most of his lectures and courses over the years were printed or recorded, so that they are still available.

Merton spoke about Christian education on a number of occasions. To understand the elements of his effective ministry as an educator, we can look at these contributions. It seems safe to say that they are giving us the essence of Merton's educational theory.

Merton on Education

When Merton decided to become a Cistercian, he put his whole heart into it, as well as the whole of his genius. He entered deeply into the Cistercian heritage and made the wisdom of the Cistercian Fathers his own. One of the Fathers with whom he seemed to develop a special affinity was Adam, the late twelfth-century novice master and later abbot of Perseigne.[2] Drawing from Adam's writings, Merton wrote an essay on "formation"—the monastic word used most frequently for education. The title is telling: "The Feast of Freedom—Monastic Formation according to Adam of Perseigne.[3] In it Merton gives his most formal statement of what he saw Christian education to be:

> To form . . . is then to draw out the inner spiritual form implanted in his soul by grace: to educate—that is to say, to "bring out" Christ in him. It is not a matter of imposing . . . a rigid and artificial form from without, but of encouraging the growth of life and the radiation of light within his soul, until this life and light gain possession of his whole being, inform all his actions with grace and liberty, and bear witness to Christ living in him. It takes account of the whole man, called to find his place in the whole Christ. It is realistic, simple, supremely spiritual; that is to say, attuned to the inspirations of the Holy Spirit. It is based on the great and fundamental truths of the Christian life—our union with Christ in His mysteries, through the mediation of Our Lady.[4]

Merton reverted to this in many ways in his writings and in his talks. It was a basic theme for him. In his last talk, given only hours before his tragic death, he said that Christianity looks

---

2. Adam, the son of a serf, was born around 1145 in Normandy. He was educated at Rheims or Sens and ordained a priest. He became a Canon Regular, then a Benedictine, and finally a Cistercian. As abbot of Perseigne he was frequently employed by the Holy See for delicate missions. He died around 1221.

3. *The Letters of Adam of Perseigne*, vol. 1, pp. 4-48.

4. *Ibid.*, p. 9.

primarily to a transformation of consciousness—a transformation and a liberation of the truth imprisoned in man by ignorance and error. . . . The traditional religions begin with the consciousness of the individual, seeking to transform and liberate the truth in each person, with the idea that it will then communicate itself to others.[5]

He then turns his attention to the educator:

Of course the man par excellence to whom this task is deputed is the monk. The monk is a man who has attained, or is about to attain, or seeks to attain, full realization. He dwells in the center of society as one who has attained realization—he knows the score . . . he has come to experience the ground of his own being in such a way that he knows the secret of liberation and can somehow or other communicate this to others.[6]

In his essay on the "Renewal of Monastic Education," Merton insisted that the "monastic life is not only *contemplative* but *prophetic.*"[7] It is to seek to live the Christian mystery with a certain fullness and obviousness that is to be a sign and an encouragement to all other Christians. Merton, then, is pointing to what is fundamental in an education, if it is to be worthy of the name *Christian;* and if the product of one's life is not Christian, how can one be truly called "Christian"? "A tree is to be judged by its fruit" (Lk 6:44). No matter what their subject be or the environment in which they are teaching it, Christian educators must be directed toward truly educating, calling forth the Christ nature that lies deep within every human person. And they can hope to do this only if they themselves

---

5. *The Asian Journal of Thomas Merton,* p. 333.

6. *Ibid.*

7. "Renewal of Monastic Education" in *Cistercian Studies,* 3 (1968): 248.

have in some way seriously moved toward full realization of themselves.

Merton is very gentle here, knowing full well the human condition. He says, "who has attained, or is about to attain, or seeks to attain." One has to "know the score" enough to know that this is the direction in which the true answers are to be found. The educator has "come to experience the ground of his own being in such a way that he knows the secret of liberation and can somehow or other communicate this to others." This is the key to the role of the educator's own "spirituality."[8]

This emphasis on the radical elements of Christian education, with its rootedness in the perduring tradition, must not be interpreted to imply a rejection of the contribution and content of modern thought. Rather, this will often be the context within which the Christian educator will be imparting true Christian education. Indeed, it is one of the great contributions the Christian educator can make: the critical and balanced acceptance of modern thought. Merton speaks of this in a talk, which he gave to fellow novice masters and to a group of abbots, the primary monastic educators:

---

8. I would like to express my reservations with regard to the word "spirituality," which I have placed in quotation marks above and here. I am a little bit afraid of the word. If, as Merton said in one of the quotes above, spirituality means being attuned to the Holy Spirit, acting in the Spirit and under his guidance, then this is fine. We ourselves are not spirits; we are very incarnate humans. We do have a spirit, but that spirit must always live and act within the context of our human existence, except for those rare moments of true transcendence when, like Paul, we do not know if we are in the body or out of the body (2 Cor 12:2). But we certainly do not want to restrict our spiritual life or our spirituality to such transcendent moments. Indeed, they are not, properly, even the goal of such a life. The goal is love. Such moments certainly do nurture true love of God and all fellow humans, who in such moments are truly experienced in their participation in him. Our "spiritual life" must be seen to be our real life, the fullness of human life, open to all that we are and are called to be. "Spirituality" is a way of coming to integration, of gaining the freedom to be who we are and to act out of that reality. With that understanding I will use the word—still fearful that the reader might want to make his or her spirituality a *part* of life's *dimension*, instead of the very *fabric*, the *whole substance*, of life.

In opening our minds to modern thought (and, after all, this means recognizing that we too are "moderns") we must also realize its limitations, and its own peculiar hazards. Above all, we must be aware of its complexities, its variations, its confusions, since "modern thought" is not a harmonious unity. Modern man is not in agreement with himself. He has not one voice to listen to, but a thousand voices, a thousand ideologies, all competing for his attention in a babel of tongues. Our responsibility to modern man goes far beyond playing games with him, learning some of his lingo in order to tell him what we imagine he wants to hear. Our responsibility to him begins within ourselves. We must recognize that his problems are also ours, and stop imagining that we live in a totally different world. We must recognize that our common problems are not solved merely by logical answers, still less by official pronouncements. Yet in taking the modern temper seriously we must not accept all its myths and illusions without questions, or we will end up by echoing slogans without meaning, substituting sociology, psychoanalysis, existentialism and Marxism for the message of the Gospel. We must use the insights of modern thought, but without deceiving ourselves.[9]

Some Practical Orientations

How, then, do we practically cultivate an integral spirituality—one that will make us true Christian educators, according to the Western contemplative tradition?

As Christians, we share with our Jewish brothers and sisters the great privilege of being sons and daughters of the Book.

---

9. "Monastic Vocation and Modern Thought" in *Monastic Studies*, 4 (1966): 17-18.

We have received the revelation and have been called forth by it to be "a chosen people, a royal priesthood, a nation set apart" (1 Pt 2:9) to be specially taught by God. The essence of all Christian spirituality has to lie in hearing the word of God and keeping it; that is, responding to the reality it opens out to us.

First, we must hear the word of God—truly *hear* it. In his above quoted essay on Adam, Merton says:

> His knowledge of Scripture, far from being mere piety or dry pedantry, entered deeply into the very substance of his everyday life, so that, like St. Bernard, Adam viewed and experienced everything in a scriptural atmosphere. He heard God's word in everything that happened. He was one who saw all things . . . centered in the mystery of Christ. Because of this unity of outlook, Adam's theology of the spiritual life is not merely a collection of devout abstractions or a synthesis of ideas; it is a *sapientia,* a wisdom which is rooted in life.[10]

Our Christian spirituality begins when we let ourselves be formed by sacred scripture and let that "mind" be in us which was in Christ Jesus (Phil 2:5). For this to become a reality, a daily encounter with the Lord in the scriptures becomes essential. I would like, then, to share with you a very simple, practical and traditional way of doing this. This method is based on monastic practice, which goes back at least to the fourth century.

First, we take our Bible. We should always treat our Bible with great reverence. It should not be simply put on the shelf with other books or tossed on the desk. It should be enthroned in our home, in our room, in our office. In many churches today the sacred text is given a special place, sometimes with a lamp burning before it, proclaiming a real Presence—for

10. *The Letters of Adam of Perseigne,* p. 8.

God is truly present in his word, waiting to speak to his people.

Method of Sacred Reading

We begin this method of sacred reading, of encounter with the Lord, by taking our Bible and reverencing it. We might kiss the sacred text, or kneel before it, or just hold it reverently in our hands, realizing the Presence—but let us bring our bodies into our act of homage and presence, making it a fully human act. Then, **aware of the presence, we call upon the Holy Spirit**, who dwells in us and who inspired the sacred rext, to help us to hear the Lord as he now speaks to us through this text.

Now we begin to **listen to the Lord speaking through the text**. It is not a question of reading so much as of listening, letting God speak to us through the words. No rush. We set aside a bit of time for this—ten or fifteen minutes, or more; whatever we can afford. We don't press on to finish a page or a chapter or even a paragraph, but rather listen and respond as we are moved. If our Lord speaks to us powerfully in the first word or sentence, we stay there and let the conversation unfold. We are not seeking knowledge, we are seeking communion.

At the end of the time we have allotted ourselves for this meeting with the Lord **we thank him**. It is really wonderful that we can get the Lord of heaven and earth to sit down with us whenever we wish and to speak to us. The scriptures are a great gift of presence for which we can never thank the Lord enough. **And we take a word with us** from the listening; not necessarily a single word, but a word, a phrase, a sentence, a thought that he has given us. Some days he will speak a word with power and we will not have to take it, it will have been given to us. Such a word might well abide with us as long as we live. Other days we will have to choose a word. If each day one of his words of life goes with us and becomes a part of our lives, or our response to life, we will come to have the "mind" of Christ—his outlook toward life and all that is.

To sum up, then, this very simple method for daily encounter with the Lord in scripture:

1. We take our Bible, come into the Presence, do reverence, and ask for the help of the Holy Spirit, who is dwelling in us.

2. We listen to the Lord speaking to us through the words of scripture for ten minutes (or whatever time we decide to give him).

3. We thank him for being with us and take a word along with us.

Centering Prayer

Certainly, it is not enough to know God conceptually. Even as we begin to know him in this way, we cannot but be attracted to him. Affections will come forth, and they will lead us to seek an ever fuller union of knowledge in and through love. An insatiable desire will begin to grow in us. If we wish to respond to it, the way leads to experiential or contemplative prayer, to going beyond our thoughts and feelings to the deeper levels of our being. Merton speaks much of this, and obviously out of lived experience:

Unless we discover this deep self, which is hidden with Christ in God, we will never really know ourselves as persons. Nor will we know God. For it is by the door of this deep self that we enter into the spiritual knowledge of God.[11]

---

11. *The New Man*, p. 32.

The fact is, however, that if you descend into the depths of your own spirit . . . and arrive somewhere near the center of what you are, you are confronted with the inescapable truth that, at the very root of your existence, you are in constant and immediate and inescapable contact with the infinite power of God.[12]

. . . an immediate existential union with him in our souls as the source of our physical life . . . an immediate existential union with the Triune God as the source of the grace and virtue in our spirit.[13]

This perfect union is not a fusion of natures but a unity of love and of experience. The distinction between the soul and God is no longer experienced as a separation into subject and object when the soul is united to God.[14]

Underlying the subjective experience of the individual self there is the immediate experience of self-consciousness. It is completely non-objective. It has in it none of the split and alienation that occurs when the subject becomes aware of itself as a quasi-object. The consciousness of Being . . . is an immediate experience that goes beyond reflexive awareness. It is not "consciousness of" but *pure consciousness,* in which the subject as such "disappears."[15]

The dynamics of emptying and of transcendence accurately define the transformation of the Christian consciousness in Christ.[16]

---

12. *The Contemplative Life,* p. 28.
13. *The New Man,* pp. 84 and 85.
14. *A Thomas Merton Reader,* p. 515.
15. *Zen and the Birds of Appetite,* pp. 63-64.
16. *Ibid.,* p. 75.

The charity that is poured forth in our hearts by the Holy Spirit brings us into an intimate experiential communion with Christ.[17]

A man cannot enter into the deepest center of himself and pass through the center into God unless he is able to pass entirely out of himself and empty himself and give himself to other people in the purity of selfless love.[18]

This going beyond thought and concepts may seem like a very mysterious and difficult thing. Actually it is not. It is quite simple—simple, but not easy, in the sense that it calls for stepping out in faith.

Through all recorded history, among the classical religious traditions, we find men and women turning to the masters of their tradition, seeking guidance in the quest of the true self, of the true meaning of life, of the transcendence that will alone satisfy the infinite longings of the human heart. For us Christians this has been a quest to be who we are as men and women baptized into Christ and brought into the inner life of the Trinity. It is a quest to experience our true being in God, our true oneness with him.

In his thought and his practice, Merton draws upon the earliest of Christian traditions, the Fathers of the Desert. In the fourth century, as in ours, men and women set forth toward the East to find spiritual teaching. These early Christians turned to the spiritual fathers and mothers in the deserts of Egypt, Syria and Asia Minor. From thence they brought back to the West, to be disseminated by the monastics through the ensuing centuries, the teachings on prayer that these fathers and mothers had learned from their fathers and mothers. This

---

17. *No Man Is an Island*, p. 137.
18. *New Seeds of Contemplation*, p. 64.

living tradition goes on. Merton learned it from his spiritual fathers at Gethsemani and shared it in his writings.

We have sought to share it more widely through a simple method which has received the popular name of "centering prayer"—inspired by Merton's insistence upon going to the center. Like the method for sacred reading, it can be summed up in three points:

1. At the beginning of the prayer we take a minute or two to quiet down and then move in faith and love to God dwelling in our depths; at the end of the prayer we take a couple of minutes to come out, mentally praying the Our Father or some other prayer.

2. After resting for a bit in the center in faith-full love, we take up a single, simple word that expresses our being to God in love and begin to let it repeat itself within.

3. Whenever in the course of the prayer we become aware of anything else, we simply, gently return to the Presence by the use of our prayer word.

Let me add just a few words of explanation here. The whole essence of the prayer is in the first movement, a turning to God in love. The rest of the method is to enable us to remain with him peacefully. By faith we know that the Lord dwells in us: "If anyone loves me, he will keep my commandments. And my Father will love him and we will come and dwell in him" (Jn 14:24). For a moment we recall this indwelling and respond to the Lord dwelling in us with love. We rest with him. We give ourselves to him. We want to stay with him for these minutes, let everything else go by and give him a chance to reveal himself to us. As lovers, again and again we breathe his name, or whatever our little word we use says to us: I am all yours. I love you. You are mine. The word may be his name:

Jesus, Lord, God, Father, Love. Whatever it is, it is a most intimate expression of love. We do not necessarily repeat it constantly, as one might a mantra, but we use it only as we need it, only as it spontaneously reaffirms and intensifies our being to our Beloved in love.

But alas, our interior TV simply will not turn off. Very soon, perhaps, and perhaps again and again, we are drawn away from the Presence by some mundane affair, by our wandering desires or fears or concerns. No harm done. As soon as we become aware of this, we simply and most gently return to the Presence with the use of our prayer word. Each time we do this, it is a pure act of love, a real option for the Lord, and a growing detachment from the things that have tended to pull us away from him.

It is important for us not to judge the quality of our prayer by the presence or absence of thoughts or the use of the word, or indeed anything else. There is no place for judgment here. We are simply spending some time with our Beloved. What happens, happens. The important thing is that we are making time for him, giving ourselves to him. We are not there to get anything for ourselves, especially not some sort of self-satisfaction or feelings of peace or the like. This is a very pure and Christian prayer. It is a real dying to self to give ourself in love to God.

To those first learning this prayer we suggest that they try to set aside twenty minutes for it, and to find a place where they are not likely to be disturbed during that time. Most people find twenty minutes a good period. The stresses and strains of the day fall away, and we are refreshed in the Lord. Two periods a day, though, are certainly far better than one. Our aim, of course, is not just to have some periods of good prayer—as important and blessed as this might be. What we are seeking is that transformation of consciousness, leading to a wholly centered life, to constant prayer; that is, to a state where we are always coming out of the center and always resting in God's love. Are twenty minutes twice a day and ten minutes more for the meeting with the Lord in scripture—less than an hour—too much to give ourselves for cultivating the most important dimension of our lives?

There is a great deal more I could say to develop these three points. I have written extensively about this form of centering prayer elsewhere, and I would simply refer you to those writings, listed in this book's bibliography. What is important to be aware of is the fact that we do not know how to pray as we ought, especially when we begin to open ourselves to this deeper form of prayer. But the Holy Spirit will teach us all things (Rom 8:26). This prayer form opens us to make space and be attentive to the movement and leading of the Spirit. It would be a great mistake to try to do the prayer "right." It is, rather, making space in our lives, both in regard to time and to mental attitude and desire, to allow God to reveal to us our true selves in the eyes of his love and to bring us to the freedom of the sons and daughters of God. Some things can only be known by experience. That is true of this kind of experiential prayer. "Be still and know that I am God" (Ps 46:10). "Taste and see how sweet the Lord is" (Ps 33:9).

Through the regular practice of this sort of prayer we can come to that experience of ourselves in Christ. We will experience our true freedom in Christ, of which Merton spoke and which will enable us as educators to communicate these realities to others and lead them into an experiential knowledge of them—the goal of all true Christian education.

The Context of Joy

One of the things that made Merton such an effective educator was his great empathy. This flowed, of course, from his contemplative experience. He was deeply in touch with his own feelings, and he was deeply in touch with those of others, because of the love he had for them in Christ through his experience of oneness with them in the contemplative experience. He was not afraid to express his feelings—his love, his anger, his pain, his confusion, his bewilderment and searching, his hope, and ultimately his intense joy. He knew all the human emotions, and he knew how to express and share them. But in the end, as one who "knows the score," he held all in the context of joy. So people listened to him, as to one who knew what point they were at and who knew the answer. His abiding joy, which so constantly bubbled forth and which expressed itself in so much good humor and in appreciation of the creation, was not basically an emotional thing, nor was it idealistic or unrealistic. It was based on a true perception of reality, held firmly in faith and experienced more and more in contemplation.

Some years ago we had in our monastery a Zen retreat, what they call a *sesshein*. I do not think such an event could have taken place if Merton had not courageously shown us the way to open to the East according to the mind of the Second Vatican Council. Our "retreat master" was Josha Sasaki Roshi, an eminent Zen master from Japan. He did not know much English, so I gave him a Japanese-English New Testament, for he wanted to conduct this sesshein as a Christian-Zen retreat. He studied the scriptures with care and challenged us with many striking insights and gave us key texts for our "Koan" meditation.

On the fifth night of the retreat I had a most moving experience. I went in to see the Roshi. He sat there before me, very much a Buddha. As he smiled from ear to ear and rocked gleefully back and forth, he said: "I like Christianity. But I would not like Christianity without the resurrection." Then he added: "Show me your resurrection. I want to see your resurrection." In his simplicity and clarity, the master had gone straight to the heart of things. With his directness he was saying what everyone else implicitly says to us Christians: You are a Christian. You are risen with Christ. Show me, and I will believe.

Reality is that we are risen with Christ. Staying too much on the surface, we are all too often conscious only of the passing experiences of the disintegration of sin in our lives. It is when we stop and go to our deeper selves that we find ourselves one with Christ, the object of the infinitely caring and tender love of the Father. This is the true Christian perception. This is where Merton was. And this is why he was so effective as a Christian educator. He came out of reality. And he touched what was truest in his disciples. When they heard him, when they say him, they sensed their deepest longing, and they sensed a hope that here was someone who could lead them to find their true selves and the fulfillment of their deep, undecipherable longings. Even though Merton shared very fully the anxieties of our times—he once wrote: "I am up to my eyes in angst"—he was able to hold life constantly in the context of joy, its true context. Each day he heard in the gospels the proclamation of the good news, and in his prayer he experienced the all-affirming, creative love of God at the ground of his being, in each one of his brothers and sisters, and at the heart of the whole creation.

Merton stands as a wonderful example and a powerful witness of the potential of the western contemplative tradition to bring an educator to a personal fulfillment that will mightily empower him as an educator, as one who calls forth his students to the full realization of who they are in Christ.

The Spiritual Father:
Father Louis' Theory and Practice

Already in his earliest writings, Thomas Merton affirmed the value and importance of spiritual guidance. In the patronizing piety of *The Seven Storey Mountain,* which he later rightly disowned, he disavowed the value of the teaching he received in the Protestant Church because it was not made actual by spiritual direction.[1] More accurate perhaps was his awareness that it was a lack of guidance that left his first year as a Catholic filled with confusion and a certain amount of moral back-sliding.[2]

In May 1951, Father Louis became spiritual father of the scholastics and began to speak of "my children."[3] This seems all the more incongruous as he brings out in the same passages that these young professed monks were going through the same experiences that the thirty-six-year-old Merton went through just five years earlier.[4] But at this point in his development he was to some extent a product of the pre-Vatican Church, which had recently admitted him, and not yet the prophet of a renewed Church. It was a somewhat paternalistic Church within which spiritual direction tended to be paternalistic. Yet, one of his scholastics has assured me that this was more a matter of language than of attitude. He did not seem paternalistic in the sense of making one dependent; he made decided demands on his "sons." He was free and aimed at

---

1. *The Seven Storey Mountain,* p. 53.
2. *Ibid.,* pp. 229ff.
3. *The Sign of Jonas,* p. 329.
4. *Ibid.,* p. 335.

freedom. At the same time, if one of the young monks had a real problem he found a most sympathetic and patient father. All of this would certainly be affirmed later in the things Father Louis would say about spiritual direction in an article published in *Sponsa Regis*[5] and then republished in *Spiritual Direction and Meditation.*

Before looking at this more formal treatment of the matter, there is a good bit to be gleaned from passages in *The Sign of Jonas,* where Merton speaks of the relationship with his "children." Merton comes out of a tradition where the role of the spiritual father, when the tradition is liveliest and fullest, is held in high esteem. The Cistercians were founded to live Benedict of Nursia's *Rule for Monasteries* to the full. The Trappists to which he belonged sought with very varying degrees of success to maintain the spirit of the Cistercian founders. Saint Benedict placed at the head of his monastery an *abba,* abbot, who was to be a Christlike spiritual father to his monks.[6] If the monastery was large he would appoint deans to assist him in this task.[7] For the novices he provided a wise old man who knew how to win souls.[8] Wise old monks were also to help him in caring for the troublesome and recalcitrant.[9]

When Dom James Fox, who had been his abbot for twenty years, was about to retire, Father Louis made it very clear that he was not open to being elected abbot and to assuming the role of spiritual father of that large monastic family. But this was an older and wiser Merton, who had moved toward the eremitical life and who had in fact exercised an extensive spiritual paternity at Gethsemani, even to the extent of being the abbot's confessor.[10] In 1951 he was very happy to be

5. "Spiritual Direction" in *Sponsa Regis* (now *Sisters Today*), 30 (1959): 249-54.
6. *RB1980. The Rule of Saint Benedict,* chap. 2, pp. 170ff.
7. *Ibid.,* chap. 21, pp. 216ff.
8. *Ibid.,* chap. 58:6, pp. 266-67.
9. *Ibid.,* chap. 27:2, pp. 222-23.
10. James Fox, "The Spiritual Son" in Hart, ed., *Thomas Merton, Monk—A*

appointed spiritual father of the scholastics or young professed monks. And in 1955 he was eager to move on to be
father of the novices, an office he held for ten years.[11] Thus he
held within his community the two offices under abbot which
most implied the service of spiritual paternity.

Spiritual Father of the Scholastics

But let us return to Merton in the early fifties and *The Sign
of Jonas*. In his various reflections on his new role as spiritual
father of the scholastics, Father Louis gives us some insight
into the elements he saw within the role of spiritual paternity.

First of all the spiritual father is a listener; he provides space,
is open and lets people reveal themselves. Merton as spiritual
father of the scholastics continued to spend many hours in his
work room, but now in addition to writing (he wrote *No Man
Is an Island* during this period) and translating he listened and
learned. He came to reverence these young men: "The more I
get to know my scholastics the more reverence I have for their
individuality."[12] It is very important for a spiritual father to
realize that each is a unique individual. What worked well for
the father might not be the answer for the son. "This is to me
both a confusion and an education—to see that they can
mostly get along quite well without what I used to think I
needed."[13]

The listening of the spiritual father is not a passive thing; it
is very active. Merton expresses it beautifully: "I have looked
into their hearts . . . ,"[14] and he adds another important aspect
of this role, one which the concept of spiritual father, with its

---

Monastic Tribute, p. 144. Fox says of Merton that he was "a gifted director of
others in the spiritual life."

11. *Ibid.*, pp. 149ff.
12. *The Sign of Jonas*, p. 337.
13. *Ibid.*
14. *Ibid.*, p. 330.

implied loving, responsible relationship, seems to evoke more than that of spiritual director, ". . . and taken up their burdens upon me."[15] In accepting this service, the spiritual father knows that his love must be such that the disciples' suffering, wounds and needs become his own. I remember one of the great spiritual fathers on Mount Athos telling me that he considered his most important service as spiritual father to stand before the icon of Christ and mystically visit his sons in the night.

In questioning the effectiveness of his service, Merton brings out what he saw to be the goals of spiritual direction:

> I do not know if they have discovered anything new or if they are able to love God more, or if I have helped them find themselves, which is to say to lose themselves.[16]

Merton was convinced of the teaching role of the spiritual father: "I constantly preach to them from the encyclicals that they must know theology."[17] He himself though was in a learning mode:

> I have discovered that after all what they most need is not conferences on mysticism but more light about the ordinary virtues whether they be faith or prudence, charity or temperance, hope or justice or fortitude. And above all what they need and what they desire is to penetrate the Mystery of Christ and to know him in his Gospels and in the whole Bible.[18]

---

15. *Ibid*. One of the monk-priests who was a scholastic at that time attests that he was certainly highly gifted for active listening and made one feel listened to.
16. *Ibid.*, p. 333.
17. *Ibid.*, p. 337.
18. *Ibid.*

What is most important in Merton's growing understanding is the insight he expresses in the prologue to *The Sign of Jonas*:

> I found in writing The Ascent to Truth that technical language, though it is universal and certain and accepted by theologians, does not reach the average man and does not convey what is most personal and vital in religious experience.[19]

Thus he shifted his focus from talking about dogmas in themselves and rather tried to bring out "their repercussions in the life of the soul in which they begin to find concrete realization."[20] This is the kind of theology of learning, that he as a spiritual father wanted to bring to his sons, and for two purposes: to enable them to love God more—the obvious first purpose of everything—and to help them find their true selves.

Merton would later explore this notion of "self" very extensively, challenged and enlightened by psychology, the behavorial sciences, and the spirituality of the East. As the young Merton penned these lines, I doubt that he had any inkling of what was to come. In spiritual guidance we do seek to help one to discover the true self, the image of God entirely one with him whom it images, the child of God baptized into an inconceivable oneness with the very Son of God. As Merton here states, the discovery of this true self is at the same time the loss of the false self, the self we in our folly have created to distinguish ourselves from God and from our fellows, the self that requires defensiveness and begets competition, envy, jealousy and fear.

Merton, who was a man of quick and deep perception, knew right from the start that "the one who is going to be most formed by the new scholasticate is the Master of Scholastics."[21]

---

19. Ibid., p. 9.
20. *Ibid.*
21. *Ibid.*, p. 330.

It is something in the ordinary providence of God that when he uses us for others he intends to make us the greater beneficiaries. Christ came and died "for us and for our salvation," but rightly he receives the greater glory out of being our Savior. God can use us as unwilling and unprofiting instruments for the benefit of others. But if we enter lovingly into his plan, we will benefit by all that he gives to others through us.

Since *The Sign of Jonas* is a personal journal, it is not surprising that we hear more of what Merton himself got out of his ministry than of the ministry itself. But this is important to hear. The candidness of some of these passages is what is most touching and attractive in Merton's journaling.

> Their [his "children's"] calmness will finally silence all that remains of my own turbulence. . . . They refresh me with their simplicity. . . . I make resolutions to speak less wildly, to say fewer of the things that surprise myself and them.[22]

He found his ministry a stimulus to live more faithfully: "I am obliged to live the rule in order to talk about it."[23] In his ministry he accepted his failures:

> I have not always seen clearly and I have not carried their burdens too well and I have stumbled around a lot and on many days we have gone around in circles and fallen into ditches because the blind were leading the blind.[24]

He saw his temptations in a positive light, "to learn how to help all the other ones who would be one way or another tempted."[25] He was confronted by his limitations:

---

22. *Ibid.*, p. 338.
23. *Ibid.*, p. 229.
24. *Ibid.*, p. 333.
25. *Ibid.*, p. 229.

On all sides I am confronted by questions I cannot answer, because the time for answering them has not yet come. Between the silence of God and the silence of my own soul stands the silence of the souls entrusted to me. Immersed in these three silences, I realize that the questions I ask myself about them are perhaps no more than a surmise.[26]

But in all this, Father Louis found fulfillment. Most surprisingly for him and for us, at least for a time he found fulfillment even of his greatest desire, the desire for solitude:

All this experience replaced my theories of solitude. I do not need a hermitage, because I have found one where I least expected it. It was when I knew my brothers less well that my thoughts were more involved in them. Now that I know them better, I can see something of the depths of solitude which are in every human person, but which most men do not know how to lay open either to themselves, or to others or to God.[27]

And again: "I know what I have discovered: that the kind of work I once feared because I thought it would interfere with 'solitude' is in fact the only path to solitude."[28] But he adds: "One must be in some sense a hermit before the care of souls can serve to lead one further into the desert."[29]

Spiritual Direction and Meditation

Let us leave *The Sign of Jonas* for the moment and turn to Merton's first formal treatment on spiritual direction. As I

---

26. *Ibid.*, p. 344.
27. *Ibid.*, p. 337.
28. *Ibid.*, p. 333.
29. *Ibid.*

have said earlier in this chapter, it first appeared in a periodical for religious women and later was incorporated in a greatly expanded form in a little book entitled *Spiritual Direction and Meditation*. The article was written for the Christian, especially the religious, seeking direction, rather than for the director, although Merton hoped by it to encourage the average priest to venture into some direction in the administration of the sacrament of reconciliation.[30] This ties in with his later note that direction is not necessary for all; those who do not have a special vocation or mission in the Church should be able to get enough "direction" in the course of ordinary Christian life with its family and community interaction and the sacraments.[31]

Merton makes it clear why he undertook to write on spiritual direction; he wants to dispel over-rigid and stereotypical ideas.[32] He is here as everywhere in his later years a champion of freedom, full humanness and personal responsibility. When he comes to speak of the necessity of spiritual direction, he maintains that it is absolutely necessary for young religious. The reason he gives might surprise us: to safeguard them against deformation.[33] Merton shows himself as the true son of the author of the *Apologia* when he unleashes his ironical pen against authoritarian rigidity:

It assumes as a basic axiom of the spiritual life that every soul needs to be humiliated, frustrated and beaten down; that all spontaneous aspirations are suspect by the very fact that they are spontaneous; that everything individual is to be cut away, and that the soul is to be reduced to a state of absolute, machine-like conformity with others in the same fantastic predicament. Result: a

---

30. *Spiritual Direction and Meditation,* Preface.
31. *Ibid.,* p. 13.
32. *Ibid.,* Preface.
33. *Ibid.,* p. 15.

procession of robot "victim souls" moving jerkily from exercise to exercise in the spiritual life, secretly hating the whole business and praying for an early death, meanwhile "offering it up" so that the whole may not be lost.[34]

In the preface Merton gives his description of a spiritual director:

A trusted friend who, in an atmosphere of sympathetic understanding, helps and strengthens us in our groping efforts to corrrespond with the grace of the Holy Spirit, who alone is the true Director in the fullest sense of the word.

Later in the work he underlines this subordination to the Holy Spirit:

His direction is, in reality, nothing more than a way of leading us to see and obey our real Director—the Holy Spirit, hidden in the depths of our souls.[35]

In the body of the book, Merton gives another, less descriptive definition:

A spiritual director is, then, one who helps another to recognize and to follow the inspirations of grace in his life, in order to arrive at the end to which God is leading him.[36]

But extensive descriptions are also offered:

---

34. *Ibid.*, p. 12.
35. *Ibid.*, p. 30.
36. *Ibid.*, p. 9.

The director is one who knows and sympathizes, who understands circumstances, who is not in a hurry, who is patiently and humbly waiting for indications of God's action in the soul. He is concerned . . . with the whole life of the soul. He is not interested merely in our actions. He is much more interested in the basic attitudes of our soul, our inmost aspirations, our way of meeting difficulties, our mode of responding to good and evil.[37]

The third section of Merton's essay is entitled "How to Profit by Direction." In it he notes three elements: gratitude, balanced expectations (look for kindly support, not freedom from all problems or wish of fulfillment; look for wise advice, not for all the answers) and a simple and sincere manifestation of conscience. The last he considers so central that he devotes another, longer section to it. He emphasizes that it is not the same as confession of sins. "What we need to do is bring the director into contact with our real self, as best we can, and not fear to let him see what is false in our false self."[38] This may not involve anything sinful, but it may be much more humiliating and difficult to reveal than our sins. Indeed, as Merton notes, sometimes it is more difficult to reveal the good aspirations that the Lord is inspiring in the depths of our being. "We must learn to say what we really mean in the depths of our souls, not what we think we are expected to say, not what somebody else has just said."[39]

There is a very direct reciprocity between the qualities of the director and the responsibilities of the directee.

In this treatise, Merton does distinguish in some way between the spiritual director and a spiritual father. In the opening paragraphs of the work he notes that Christian spiritual

---

37. *Ibid.*, p. 25.
38. *Ibid.*, p. 24.
39. *Ibid.*, p. 29.

direction had its origins with the spiritual fathers in the desert. Then he goes on to say:

> It must not be forgotten that the spiritual director in primitive times was much more than the present name implies. He was a spiritual father who "begot" the perfect life in the soul of his disciple by his instruction first of all, but also by his prayer, his sanctity and his example. He was to the young monk a kind of "sacrament" of the Lord's presence in the ecclesial community.[40]

I am sure that Merton would not want this to be seen as a real distinction. We must realize that the relationship between director and directee cannot always be as intimate ("The neophyte lives in the same cell with him, day and night, and did what he saw his father doing"[41]), but every good Christian spiritual director will strive to move in the direction of being a true spiritual father or mother.

Merton notes that spiritual direction is not counseling or psychotherapy. He warns against amateur attempts at the latter.[42] The director should know when to refer someone to a professional therapist. His direction is spiritual, integrating spiritual principles that have been revealed, and aiming at a fullness of life that is beyond even a fully human integration.

After forty pages of sometimes rather intricate and always very rich consideration, Merton wisely concludes by warning us not to make too much of all this. If spiritual direction for us is largely experienced as a quietly deepening friendship with a special openness and grounding, we shouldn't look for trouble or problems but rather realize that the steadiness of this special friendship is perhaps one of the main reasons why things are generally progressing peacefully for us.

---

40. *Ibid.*, p. 9.
41. *Ibid.*
42. *Ibid.*, pp. 6 and 40-41.

Spiritual Direction and Contemplatives

In 1960, Merton began a course for the priests of his monastery, entitled "An Introduction to Christian Mysticism—From the Apostolic Fathers to the Council of Trent." He "published" the lectures in a mimeograph book in August of the following year, 1961.[43] The last forty-five pages consist of two lectures on "The Spiritual Direction of Contemplatives."

The emphasis on freedom and responsibility again stands out. A director should never be imposed. When one is chosen he has no jurisdiction, no right to obedience. His authority is spiritual; it should call forth a complete docility—an ability to learn what is to be prudently applied to one's life. Learning, humility, prudence and charity are more important in a director than holiness and experience, though these, too, are very desirable qualities.

In the section of this study where Merton surveys the history of spiritual direction we get a further hint of the evolution of a broader vision. He situates the Christian history in the broader world context. He passes over "the very interesting and important topic of direction in Yoga and in Buddhism," for these had not yet captivated his interest as they soon would, but he does explore extensively the master-disciple relationship in classical philosophical schools. In the next few years his horizons would expand, as is evidenced in the 1967 volume, *Mystics and Zen Masters*.

The Wisdom of the Desert

But first his expansion and deepening would come through his increasing study of the spiritual father of the Christian

---

43. *An Introduction to Christian Mysticism—From the Apostolic Fathers to the Council of Trent*. A manuscript of lectures given at the Abbey of Gethsemani. The author's name is not given. At the end of the foreword we find the date: Vigil of the Assumption, 1961.

East. In his series of interesting taped talks, *Solitude and Community: The Paradox of Life and Prayer*, Keith Egan speaks at length of Thomas Merton:

> He began to read the literature that came out of the desert, the Christian desert of the fourth century. And one of the most important books he wrote is his shortest, and that is *The Wisdom of the Desert*. . . . The study that lies behind the writing of this little book was transforming and changed Merton's life forever.[44]

About the same time that Father Louis was giving his lectures on spiritual direction to his fellow monks, he put together this little collection of the sayings of the Fathers of the Desert. These he first published in the rather exclusive edition, *What Ought I To Do? Sayings of the Desert Fathers*, prepared by his friend Victor Hammer. However, they soon came out in the popular edition, *The Wisdom of the Desert*, mentioned by Egan. In the twenty-two-page introductory essay Merton never uses the term "spiritual direction" and says relatively little of the relationship between the spiritual fathers or elders and their disciples. It is, rather, the quiet, ever-present context of the whole. Statements in the essay are important, indicating the evolution and thrust of Merton's thought, which would profoundly affect his approach to spiritual direction.

> The society they sought was one where all men were truly equal, where the only authority under God was the charismatic authority of wisdom, experience and love. . . . What the Fathers sought most of all was their own true self, in Christ.[45]

He could not retain the slightest identification with his

---

44. Keith Egan, *Solitude and Community: The Paradox of Life and Prayer*, tape 3, "The Desert: Place of Discovery."

45. *The Wisdom of the Desert*, p. 5.

superficial, transient, self-constructed self. He had to lose himself in the inner, hidden reality of a self that was transcendent, mysterious, half-known, and lost in Christ.[46]

They sought a way to God that was uncharted and freely chosen, not inherited from others who had mapped it out beforehand. . . . There was nothing to which they had to "conform" except the secret, hidden, inscrutable will of God which might differ very notably from one cell to another![47]

We see a new terminology coming into Merton's vocabulary here:

The "rest" which these men sought was simply that sanity and poise of a being that no longer has to look at itself because it is carried by the perfection of freedom that is in it. And carried where? Wherever Love itself, or the Divine Spirit, sees fit to go. Rest, then, was a kind of simple no-whereness and no-mindedness that had lost all preoccupation with a false or limited "self." At peace in the possession of a sublime "nothing" the spirit laid hold, in secret, upon the "all"—without trying to know what it possessed.[48]

This terminology did not come from the *verba seniorum*, the terminology of the Fathers. A clue to its origins comes on the next page: "In many respects, therefore, these Desert Fathers had much in common with Indian Yogis and with Zen Buddhist monks of China and Japan."[49] The opening to the East through the Christian East was under way.

---

46. *Ibid.*, p. 7.
47. *Ibid.*, p. 6.
48. *Ibid.*, p. 8.
49. *Ibid.*, p. 9.

Among the essays published in 1967 in *Mystics and Zen Masters*, there is a preface Merton wrote for Segius Bolshakoff's study of the *Russian Mystics*. As this book's publication was delayed, Merton published his work as an essay under the title "Russian Mystics." In this he has a very significant statement on spiritual direction, which indicates the simplicity which his own notions on this subject had attained:

> The purpose of *Starchestvo*[50] is, then, not so much to make use of daily spiritual direction in order to inculcate a special method of prayer, but rather to keep the heart of the disciple open to love, to prevent it from hardening in self-centered concern (whether moral, spiritual or ascetical). All the worst sins are denials and rejections of love, refusals to love. The chief aim of the starets [the spiritual father] is first to teach his disciple not to sin against love, then to encourage and assist his growth in love until he becomes a saint. This total surrender to the power of love was the sole basis of their spiritual authority.[51]

In spite of the title of this volume, there is little formal consideration in it of the relationship of the Zen Master and his disciple. It is rather conveyed in a multitude of stories and sayings, scattered through the essays, which remind one constantly of the stories and sayings of the Desert Fathers. Merton notes that Zen monks (like Eastern Christian monks) "seek out a particular monastery more because of a *Roshi*, or 'venerable teacher,' who is found there, than for the sake of the community or the rule."[52] The one description of the master-disciple relation he does draw is not particularly attractive, to say the least, and does not readily offer much insight into the whole

---

50. The daily manifestation of one's thoughts to one's spiritual father.

51. *Mystics and Zen Masters*, p. 186.

52. *Ibid.*, p. 217.

rather paradoxical relationship that does exist.[53] Merton himself is at pains to state that it really cannot be understood or appreciated out of the context of a full understanding of Zen.[54] This relationship in other Buddhist traditions and among the Hindus does not feature in his writings and does not seem to have been studied by him. A very interesting set of taped talks, originally given to the monks at Gethsemani in the course of his Sunday afternoon lectures, shows his interest in the Sufi master and his mode of teaching.[55]

The Spiritual in the Desert Tradition

The final essay I want to consider here is a paper Merton distributed in mimeograph in February 1966, entitled "The Spiritual Father in the Desert Tradition."[56] This was written shortly after he embarked upon the eremitical life and moved up to the hermitage on the hill. It is in part an *apologia* for the eremitical life. However, in it we see the insights emerging in his introductory essay to *The Wisdom of the Desert* now being directly applied to spiritual direction: "Every practice, every decision, every charge in one's mode of life is to be judged in terms of . . . purity of heart, perfect charity, and *quies*, or the

---

53. ". . . interviews with the Roshi. These are deliberately humiliating and frustrating, for the spiritual master is determined to waste no time tolerating the illusions and spiritual self-gratifications that may be cherished by his disciples. If necessary, he will resort (as did famous Zen masters in the past) to slapping, kicking, and other forms of physical violence" (*ibid.*, p. 229).

54. *Ibid.*, p. 215.

55. *The Mystic Life*. Note especially tape 3, "Community Life and Spiritual Direction": "They [the Sufis] have a man around who knows the score and can tell them: here is what is happening to you, here is how you fit this into the circumstances where you live. This is what spiritual direction is. That is what the spiritual life depends on—having somebody to tell you that in the beginning. After a while you can tell yourself. In Sufism, therefore, direction is very important."

56. This was published after Merton's death in *Contemplation in a World of Action*, pp. 269-93, with some editorial changes.

tranquility of the selfless and detached spirit."[57] In the final paragraph he goes further:

> This freedom and tranquility are the "good ground" in which the seed of grace and wisdom can bring forth fruit a hundredfold. This state of purity and rest is not what one can call the "summit of perfection" whatever that may mean. It is simply the last stage of development that can be observed and discussed in logical terms. It is what John the Solitary calls "integrity," but his integrity is not the end, it is really only the *beginning* of the true spiritual (*pneumatikos*) life. "Beyond integrity is mystery which cannot be defined."[58]

There is a point beyond which the spiritual father cannot guide; he can only point to the mystery.

In this essay we note two areas where Merton shows an evolution of thought. He moves from a strongly negative attitude toward the director making severe demands to a more open position:

> In fact the Spiritual Father must of necessity be uncompromisingly severe, and make extremely difficult demands upon the disciple in order to test his vocation . . . and help him make rapid progress.[59]

He does add cautions against excess on the next page. One wonders how much influence his contact with the harsh way of the Zen master had on his opening to harshness in his own tradition, which he earlier found more repugnant.

The second area is closely related to this. Earlier he carefully distinguished between obedience due superiors and others

---

57. *The Spiritual Fathers in the Desert Tradition*, manuscript, February 1966, p. 14.
58. *Ibid.*, p. 29.
59. *Ibid.*, p. 23.

with jurisdiction or ecclesial authority and the docility due the director.[60] Now he calls for obedience. There is to be

> uncompromising and complete obedience to the de-
> mands and advice of the Spiritual Father no matter how
> disconcerting any might appear. . . . If he [the disciple]
> can put up with rough treatment, realizing the Spiritual
> Father knows what he is doing, he will rapidly come to
> a state of detachment from his own will and his own
> ego.[61]

He goes on to defend this from the charge of being blind obedience:

> This is not the blind, unreasoning and passive obedi-
> ence of one who obeys merely in order to let himself be
> "broken," but the clear-sighted, trusting obedience of
> one who firmly believes that his guide knows the true
> way to peace and purity of heart and is an interpreter
> of God's will for him. Such obedience is "blind" only in
> the sense that it puts aside its own limited and biased
> judgment; but it does so precisely because it sees that to
> follow one's own judgment in things one does not
> properly understand is indeed to walk in darkness.[62]

This would seem to limit the scope of the obedience somewhat. I must confess I am more comfortable with Father Louis'
earlier distinction, but we are confronted with a monk who
became more radical and traditional even as he became more
prophetic and evolutionary. We need to let ourselves be challenged by him.

In the light of this added authority and role, Merton does
demand more of the spiritual father:

---

60. *Spiritual Direction and Meditation,* p. 40.
61. *The Spiritual Fathers in the Desert Tradition,* p. 23.
62. *Ibid.,* pp. 24-25.

The Master must be extraordinarily humble, discerning, kind, and in no sense a despotic character. The "hard sayings" which he administers must spring from genuine kindness and concern for the interests of the disciples and not from a secret desire to dominate and exploit them for his own egotistic ends. The Master must, in other words, be himself one who is no longer in the least attracted by "superiority" or by the desire to rule and teach others.[63]

In his early work on spiritual direction, Merton urged the directee to develop the virtue of prudence to "guide himself when he cannot or need not seek guidance from another."[64] Now he resorts to an earlier monastic term, a more descriptive one: "*diacrisis*, or the discernment of spirits."[65] As we have seen, all along he has emphasized that ultimately the director is the Holy Spirit and that the human director is only to help the directee to learn how to hear the Spirit and follow his lead. For such, *diacrisis* is obviously essential. There is within us, besides the indwelling divine Spirit, our own very human spirit, and if not within us certainly close by, are the evil spirits. Discernment is necessary if we are to hear and follow the Spirit of God. Merton saw that the way for the disciple to develop this is complete openness with the spiritual father, making known to him "all that is going on in his heart." Together with him, step by step, the disciple would learn to identify the inner movements and their origins.[66]

I think what we have seen here gives sufficient sense of Merton's practice, his evolution, and his basic teaching on spiritual direction. Once he left the office of novice master in

63. *Ibid.*, p. 25.
64. *Spiritual Direction and Meditation*, p. 17.
65. *The Spiritual Fathers in the Desert Tradition*, p. 22.
66. *Ibid.*

1965, he did little in the way of giving regular direction. There are some letters—he responded generously to correspondence—which contain excellent direction.[67] But his energies now were directed to broader dialogue. Merton's growth is fascinating to watch. He grew from a late-traditional, by-the-book spiritual director to a truly traditional, generative spiritual father first of monks, then of ever widening circles and whole movements, to new currents of life in Church and society.

---

67. Some examples of this may be found in "Letters in a Time of Crisis" in *Seeds of Destruction*, pp. 237-328, and *The Hidden Ground of Love*.

The Legacy of Merton's Pilgrimage to India
South India
November 26—December 5, 1968

For those who believe in the providential ordering of things by the divine, there can be no doubt that it was indeed providential that Thomas Merton spent the last weeks of his life in Asia. It is no exaggeration to say that the week he spent in South India, including Sri Lanka, was one of the most important in his life, building, of course, on all that had gone before. In a certain way it incarnates and expresses the essence of his heritage not only to the Christian community but to the whole human family, as we seek to establish some global spiritual base on which to build world peace and a humane economic order.

Merton wrote a paper to be delivered at the Spiritual Summit Conference in Calcutta just before his flight to the south. In it he said:

> I speak as a Western monk who is pre-eminently concerned with his own monastic call and dedication. I have left my monastery to come here not just as a research scholar or even as an author (which I also happen to be). I come as a pilgrim who is anxious to obtain not just information, not just "facts" about other monastic traditions, but to drink from ancient sources of monastic vision and experience. I seek not only to learn more (quantitatively) about religion and about monastic life, but to become a better and more enlightened monk (qualitatively) myself.[1]

---

1. *The Asian Journal of Thomas Merton,* pp. 312-13.

Merton did travel as a scholar. Indeed, there is a bit of humor in this, for he was constantly lamenting the sums he had to pay for excess baggage and making plans to dispose of some of the many books he acquired—but as fast as he got rid of some he would acquire more. The fact is, though, that even in the midst of a very heavy travel schedule, meetings of all sorts, and many conferences which called for major papers on his part, he yet managed to do a phenomenal amount of reading and serious study that prepared him for his meetings with scholars and spiritual masters. He took his touring seriously and read up on the places he was visiting. He wrote copious notes and interesting comments, never losing his rich sense of humor. He must have used every minute. His sweep was too broad to be extensive in any one area of concern. But his keen mind and deep spiritual sense, coming from years of contemplative experience, enabled him to penetrate far deeper into the spiritual traditions he was exploring than most dedicated, specialized scholars. The living spiritual masters whom he encountered were generally very impressed by his understanding of their tradition.

He was also a writer. And as he journeyed, he was a writer at work, not one resting on the laurels of many best sellers. As I have just mentioned, he commented in writing on the many things he was studying and reading, seeing and hearing. He discussed ideas for future books. He captured some of his experiences in poems. And as he moved along, he wrote a journal for future publication.

But above all he was a pilgrim. His secretary, Brother Patrick Hart, confirmed this in his introduction to *The Asian Journal*, writing: "Thomas Merton's pilgrimage to Asia was an effort on his part to deepen his own religious and monastic commitment."[2] We might find this statement surprising on two scores. Anyone who has read Merton extensively would

---

2. *Ibid.*, p. xxiii.

wonder about his need to deepen his monastic commitment. The man was monk, through and through. One could hardly be more dedicated to living the monastic reality. Yet, the essence of the monastic journey is that the monk continually seek. The more he comes to know experientially what the fullness of monastic life really means the more he truly proclaims that he has not yet begun.

Stability

More surprising, though, might be the fact that this monk was on pilgrimage, especially as he was a monk who professed and followed Saint Benedict's *Rule for Monasteries*. Benedict did not speak kindly of monks who travel about, going from monastery to monastery. To counteract this "vice" he even required his monks to take a vow of stability, which Merton had done. Many have raised questions over the years, and still do, about Merton's stability. Merton's interpretation of the vow of stability, which we can find extensively spelt out in the notes from his talks to his novices on the vows, was the one commonly held today by Cistercians and other followers of Benedict.

The vow of stability means fidelity to a community. It is not to be confused with the practice of enclosure, which is the expectation that the monk find everything within the confines of the monastery and therefore not go abroad. Although Benedict did provide for an enclosure and did say that it is not expedient for a monk to go outside, he did nonetheless include in his Rule a number of chapters about monks going on journeys. The ideal is for the monk to find all within his solitude, but the ideal is always something to be striven toward in this real world, never fully attained. Benedict, a man of great reality and balance, knew that, and so did Merton, at least in his later and more mature years.

In the end, Merton passed beyond the need of the practice of enclosure. Not, however, beyond his vow of stability. It is enough to read some of his last letters. He was firmly attached to his monastery, to his monastic community and to obedience to his abbot. Abbot Flavin strongly confirms this. But Merton, in the tradition of the Cistercian Fathers, especially Saint Bernard, placed much importance on getting to know oneself. And he did indeed attain a very deep self-knowledge. In his later years he did know his needs and accepted them. His genius, his talents, his gifts needed to be called forth by a living contact with great minds, with great spiritual masters and by the richness of the world's spiritual traditions. In *The Asian Journal* he wrote:

> I think we have now reached a stage of (long overdue) religious maturity at which it may be possible for someone to remain perfectly faithful to a Christian and Western monastic commitment, and yet to learn in depth from, say, a Buddhist or Hindu discipline and experience.[3]

We do not read anywhere in Merton's writings or journals of his using Buddhist or any other Eastern disciplines. He did not play around with spiritual disciplines. We do read of great fidelity to the practices of the Cistercian tradition. But, coming to the point where he judged that Eastern disciplines might be usefully integrated into his spiritual journey, he courageously set out on a pilgrimage to explore their potential. Throughout *The Asian Journal* we find him discussing spiritual practice with the great masters he encountered. Some of these practices he leaves open for further exploration. Others he quickly decides are not going to be fruitful for him. Why complicate things, he asks. Simplicity, of which he wrote very early in his

---

3. *Ibid.*, p. 313.

own monastic journey,[4] remained ever characteristic of him in his spiritual practice. This is something quite extraordinary when we consider what a complex and rich personality he possessed.

The Pilgrim

Merton did come to South India as a pilgrim, but as a very exceptional pilgrim. Exceptional not because of his fame but because of what he was seeking and the way he was seeking it. He came as perhaps no one ever had before—as a pilgrim both to the origins of Christianity expressed in Saint Thomas, and to the origins of other great spiritual traditions expressed in Shiva and the Buddha.

As Merton winged his way into Madras, one of the first things he spotted and noted was Saint Thomas Mount. Early the next morning he made his way to the Mount to celebrate the eucharistic liturgy on the site where tradition says this disciple of the Lord gave the supreme witness of his discipleship in martyrdom. He went on to the cathedral in the Mylapore district of Madras to kneel in silent prayer at the tomb of the martyr-disciple. Artist that he was, Merton expressed the depth of his experience in aesthetical terms. Of the chapel on the Mount he wrote: "A very lovely church, so quiet, so isolated, so simple, so fresh. . . . One of the nicest things I have found in India or anywhere. I felt my pilgrimage to it was a great grace."[5] These are the qualities that appealed to Merton. For him they express primitive Christianity, pure Christianity, the Christianity he loved and wanted to be in touch with.

After kneeling at the tomb of the disciple, Merton traveled along the coast to the great Shivite temple at Mahabalipurna. Later he would cite this and Polonnaruwa, of which I shall

---

4. See chapter above "Father Louis' First Book: *The Spirit of Simplicity*."

5. *The Asian Journal*, p. 196.

speak shortly, as the high points in the other dimension of his pilgrimage. However, he did have some difficulty in experiencing Mahabalipurna in the way he wanted, because of the noisy crowds and especially the pesty hawkers, who wanted to sell him postcards and show him around the impressive complex. He managed to escape from them, and in the small temple by the sea he was able to enter into the creative mystery of mother ocean lapping the great phallus, the central symbol of the Shivite temple. Out of the perfect circle, the completeness of God, comes forth this powerful burst of life, which impregnates the whole of creation, creation becoming ever more pregnant, as it approaches again and again, in greatest intimacy, the tumescent intrusion of the divine into his creation.

Three days later Merton flew to Colombo. The next morning he took an early train up into the hills to Kandy, the ancient capital of Ceylon. It was Saturday, and the weekend was largely taken up with visits to the bishop, the seminarians, and the monks at Ampitiya, although he did find time to visit with a German Buddhist monk. On Monday, Merton drove with the vicar general of the diocese to visit Dambulla and Polonnaruwa. The following day, December 3, he began the final lap of his journey to the place where a week later he would complete his earthly pilgrimage and leave for the heavenly country. Merton did not immediately write of the experience he had on Monday. Two days later he would note: "Polonnaruwa was such an experience that I could not write hastily of it and cannot write now, or not at all adequately."

At Polonnaruwa, while the disinterested vicar general hung back, Merton was able to enter into the sanctuary with the solitariness he wanted. The pilgrim took off his shoes and let the dampness of the living earth speak to him. At this point it is not only best but necessary to let Merton speak for himself:

> I am able to approach the Buddhas barefoot and undisturbed, my feet in wet grass, wet sand. Then the silence

of the extraordinary faces. The great smiles. Huge and yet subtle. Filled with every possibility, questioning nothing, knowing everything, rejecting nothing, the peace not of emotional resignation but of Madhyamika,[6] of sunyata,[7] that has seen through every question without trying to discredit anyone or anything—*without refutation*—without establishing some argument. For the doctrinaire, the mind that needs well-established positions, such peace, such silence, can be frightening. I was knocked over with a rush of relief and thankfulness at the *obvious* clarity of the figures, the clarity and fluidity of shape and line, the design of the monumental bodies composed into the rock shape and landscape, figure, rock and tree. And the sweep of bare rock sloping away on the other side of the hallow, where you can go back and see different aspects of the figures. Looking at these figures I was suddenly, almost forcibly, jerked clean out of the habitual, half-tied vision of things, and an inner clearness, clarity, as if exploding from the rocks themselves, became evident and obvious. The queer *evidence* of the reclining figure, the smile, the sad smile of Ananda standing with arms folded (much more "imperative" than Da Vinci's Mona Lisa because completely simple and straightforward). The thing about all this is that there is no puzzle, no problem, and really no "mystery." All problems are resolved and everything is clear, simply because what matters is clear. The rock, all matter, all life, is charged with dharmakaya . . . everything is emptiness and everything is compassion. I don't know when in my life I have ever had such a sense of beauty and spiritual validity running together in one

---

6. Madhyamika: the "Middle Path" school of Buddhism.

7. Sunyata: Sanskrit, "emptiness, the Void"—a basic concept in Buddhism, especially in the Madhuamika and Zen schools.

aesthetic illumination. Surely, with Mahabalipuram and Polonnaruwa my Asian pilgrimage has come clear and purified itself. I mean, I know and have seen what I was obscurely looking for. I don't know what else remains, but I have now seen and have pierced through the surface and have got beyond the shadow and the disguise.[8]

As on Mount Saint Thomas, so it is also here through the aesthetic experience that Merton entered into and sought to express the mystical experience. The same qualities stand out: quiet, isolation, simplicity and freshness. There is a wholeness. Merton said he could not express it adequately. He might have added, as did his Cistercian Fathers in speaking of such moments of total integration, that those who have experienced it know what he was talking about, and those who have not should seek the experience so that they will know.

Merton did not return to this experience in the few journal entries that would follow. As I have said, a week later he would be dead. What we do find in the following entries and in some of those that go before might surprise us. On the next page, Merton is recounting trivial events from the local newspaper. On preceding ones we find him commenting on the "comics"—including an old favorite, Tarzan. He is frequently taken up in these final days with quite ordinary sightseeing and touring. In Colombo he tries out the different bars and stays in the most luxurious hotel—this champion of social justice who could hardly have missed the surrounding abysmal poverty.[9] His delightful poem coming from the train ride up to Kandy is teeming with life of all kinds, not omitting graceful girls and bathing women. As he comes down from

8. *Ibid.*, pp. 233-36.

9. When I took a native friend to dinner at the Galle Face Hotel, the hotel in which Merton stayed, the friend remarked that what we spent for the meal equaled the average worker's monthly wage.

Mount Saint Thomas, he buys the *Selected Poems* of D. H. Lawrence, which he will read and quote for us. In Madras he discusses Blake with Dr. Raghavan. He reads again Hesse's *Steppenwolf*. He enjoys very fine, "really splendid" hotels, flying first class, good food and strong Bloody Marys. He found time for the movies. What kind of mystic is this, what kind of completion? The most complete kind.

Merton had made a long journey. He had pursued and tasted most of the desecrating pleasures of human life in his early days. He had been called forth by many causes. Then he turned his back on the pleasures and the causes to seek that ascetical path which in this hour of completion we might expect him to be deeply immersed in. But he had learned a deeper asceticism, that of total response to God in all his manifestations. It was an asceticism that left no room for posturing, for creating an image. For the clean, all things are clean. Merton was washed clean; he had attained true simplicity. He had it all together, at least for moments like Polonnaruwa, and he had most of it together most of the time in these last days. A simplicity of lack could never belong to this extraordinarily rich and complex person. He could only pursue the integration of the totally rich, divine simplicity, a simplicity that brought all to harmony in the appreciation of its participated divineness.

On the same day that Merton wrote of his experience in the presence of the Buddhas at Polonnaruwa he wrote to me from Singapore about the last book he personally prepared for the press, *The Climate of Monastic Prayer*. This is a very special book. Merton had begun to write it as an essay a number of years earlier. It was being written for his brothers and sisters in the Cistercian order. In it he shared a more personal and intimate glimpse of the contemplative prayer he himself experienced in the later years of his journey. On the last two pages he wrote:

Prayer must penetrate and enliven every department of our life, including that which is most temporal and transient. Prayer does not despise even the seemingly lowliest aspects of man's temporal existence. It spiritualizes all of them and gives them a divine orientation. . . . The most important need in the Christian world today is this inner truth nourished by this Spirit of contemplation.[10]

Merton's Heritage

This is Merton's heritage, not only to the Christian world, but to the whole human family, a heritage of integration and spiritual freedom. A long-time Indian friend, whom Merton spent some time with in Calcutta, Amiya Chakravarty, wrote that "Merton never quite accepted the fixed medieval line between the sacred and the profane."[11] Perhaps he did accept it for a time in his early days at Gethsemani, but it did violence to his nature. With the help of the Greek Fathers, especially Gregory of Nyssa, he moved back toward integration.[12] He came to see grace and nature working in harmony. He came to appreciate that grace can and does manifest itself in all creation, in all cultures, in all religions. In the paper he read on the day of his death he said: "The combination of the natural techniques and the graces and the other things that have been manisfested in Asia and the Christian liberty of the gospel should bring us all at last to that full and transcendent liberty."[13] His long quest and his open exposure to these elements did bring him to that freedom.

Writing just a month before his death from New Delhi,

10. *The Climate of Monastic Prayer*, pp. 153-54.
11. *The Asian Journal*, p. viii.
12. See chapter above "Thomas Merton and Byzantine Spirituality."
13. *The Asian Journal*, p. 343.

Merton expressed a heartfelt desire: "I hope I can bring back to my monastery something of the Asian wisdom with which I am fortunate to be in contact." He was not able to do that, except through his written words and his photographs. But through them, and far more through his lived example, so crystallized in those last days in South India, he has left, not only to his monastery but to all of us, a heritage that invites us with attractive cogency to enter into a new freedom. He calls us to fully enjoy the creative, loving presence of our God in all things, so that they in and through their reality may lead us into a new transcendent freedom.

Thomas Merton—A Historic
Reality and Challenge

Monasticism as a historical fact can be seen in a static way: as monasticism existing in any particular moment in history; or in an evolutionary way: monasticism as it evolves through the course of history. The beginnings, if we are considering monasticism in itself and not just in its Christian expression, is lost in pre-historic mists. The end of our study can be no earlier than this morning. Yesterday's monasticism is now historic monasticism, a part of history. This more recent historic monasticism is for us perhaps the more important, because through it all the richness of the earlier monastic history is mediated, albeit at times in a very diminished form. If we study the earlier monastic realities, it is precisely to fill up that diminishment, to flesh out and inspirit the fullness of our heritage.

Perhaps no monk challenges us to see this more clearly than Thomas Merton. He challenges us to see it not only by his historic and prophetic writings but especially by his own striking personal evolution. Perhaps Merton's greatest contribution is the answer he gives to us to a question that is most important not only for monks but for all the people of God: What is a monk?[1] That it is an essential question for monks is most obvious. But to underline its importance even for the whole Church I can appeal to authority. The Second Vatican Council has said:

---

1. Whenever in this chapter (as elsewhere throughout this book) I speak of monks I mean also nuns. We do not yet have a satisfactory inclusive word. (Dom Jean Leclercq suggested "nunks"!) I do not particularly care for the use of "monastic" as a substantive.

The monastic life, that venerable institution which in the course of a long history has won for itself notable renown in the Church and in human society, should be preserved with care and its authentic spirit permitted to shine forth ever more splendidly both in the East and in the West.[2]

The history of the human family attests to this. Almost every major religious tradition has had at its heart as a barometer of its vitality a monastic core of men and women totally dedicated to the way.

Merton does of course not attempt to give an absolute definition of the monk or of monastic life. It is a living, growing phenomenon. He circles it and describes it with great richness. He highlights its many facets. He challenges its present historical expressions to grow and evolve. What he has to say about the monk and monastic life will not give us the full answer for today; but it will give us a good starting point to move on to the articulation of who monks are and how they ought to live the monastic life, as we move out of centuries of history into the twenty-first century.

As I mentioned above, what is most instructive and interesting in Merton is the evolution of his own monastic consciousness. To bring this out, I want to limit myself to considering some of his earliest expressions and some of his last reflections on the monastic reality.

The Young Monk

The Seven Storey Mountain was written after Merton had been in the monastic life for about six or seven years. It undoubtedly reflects his thinking at the time of writing as well as his thinking at earlier periods, insofar as he was able to

2. Decree on the Adaptation and Renewal of Religious Life, #9.

reconstruct it. It is also, I believe, a fairly accurate expression of the common understanding of the time, though with perhaps a bit more poetry and idealism than the average devout Catholic could muster. Let's listen to a few passages:

> What wonderful happiness there was, then, in the world. There were still men on this miserable, noisy, cruel earth, who tasted the marvelous joy of silence and solitude, who dwelt in forgotten mountain cells, in secluded monasteries where the news and desires and appetites and conflicts of the world no longer reached them.
>
> They were free from the burden of the flesh's tyranny, and their clear vision, clean of the world's smoke and of its bitter sting, were raised to heaven and penetrated into the deeps of heaven's infinite and healing light.
>
> They were poor, they had nothing, and therefore they were free and possessed everything, and everything they touched struck off something of the fire of divinity. And they worked with their hands, silently ploughing and harrowing the earth, and sowing seed in obscurity, and reaping their small harvests to feed themselves and the other poor. They built their own houses and made, with their own hands, their own furniture and their own course clothing, and everything around them was simple and primitive and poor, because they were the least and the last of men, they had made themselves outcasts, seeking, outside the walls of the world, Christ poor and rejected of men.
>
> Above all, they had found Christ, and they knew the power and the sweetness and the depths and the infinity of His love, living and working in them. In Him, hidden in Him, they had become the "Poor Brothers of God."

And for His love, they had thrown away everything,
and concealed themselves in the Secret of His Face. Yet,
because they had nothing, they were the richest men in
the world, possessing everything: Because in proportion as grace emptied their hearts of created desire, the
Spirit of God entered in and filled the place that had
been made for God. And the Poor Brothers of God, in
their cells, they tasted within them the secret glory, the
hidden manna, the infinite nourishment and strength of
the Presence of God. They tasted the sweet exultancy of
the fear of God, which is the first intimate touch of the
reality of God, known and experienced on earth, the
beginning of heaven.[3]

Hints of the later Merton are not wholly absent from this early
idealism. There was concern about the person, as seen in this
passage:

And yet, what a strange admission! To say that men
were admirable, worthy of honor, perfect, in proportion
as they disappeared into a crowd and made themselves
unnoticed, by even ceasing to be aware of their own
existence and their own acts. Excellence, here, was in
proportion to obscurity: The one who was best was the
one who was least observed, least distinguished. Only
faults and mistakes drew attention to the individual. . . .

But what was the answer to this paradox? Simply that
the monk in hiding himself from the world becomes not
less himself, not less of a person, but more of a person,
more truly and perfectly himself: For his personality
and individuality are perfected in their true order, the

---

3. *The Seven Storey Mountain*, pp. 316-17. *The Seven Storey Mountain* is certainly
not our only source for the monastic thought of Merton during these early
days, but it is consistent with the rest.

spiritual, interior order, of union with God, the principle of all perfection.[4]

There was a certain social awareness in his life at that time. How could there not have been, considering his past. In those last days before he entered the monastery, his life was profoundly touched by the Baroness de Hueck. He spent hot summer nights at Friendship House sharing with her and her followers and monitoring the activities of the young people brought in off the streets of Harlem.

Back at college he questioned the reality of the lives of the Sisters who flocked about the campus at summer school: "Was the relative comfort of their life apt to make them impervious to certain levels of human experience and human misery?"[5] But the most significant thing he saw about the Baroness at this time was that she "could gather around her souls like these holy women and could form, in her organization, others that were, in the same way, saints, whether white or colored."[6] If she could continue to do this, Merton was sure "she would not only have won her way, but she might eventually, by the grace of God, transfigure the face of Harlem."[7]

This, for Merton, was the important thing. And notwithstanding his reflections in regard to the Sisters on campus, it seemed to him, "It was right, of course, that my interior life should have been concerned first of all with my own salvation: it must be that way."[8] He does go on to say: "But now it was necessary that I take more account of obligations to other men, born of the very fact that I was myself a man among men, and a sharer in their sins and in their punishments and in their

---

4. *Ibid.*, p. 330.
5. *Ibid.*, p. 338.
6. *Ibid.*, p. 348.
7. *Ibid.*
8. *Ibid.*, p. 339.

miseries and in their hopes. No man goes to heaven all by himself, alone."[9] But as he moves on, his response is essentially the common one of contemplative monks of that period: "When you consider the effect of individual merit upon the vitality of other members of the Mystical Body, it is evident that there is nothing sterile about contemplation."[10] In the final pages of *The Seven Storey Mountain* he goes through an elaborate argumentation about the merit of the different forms of religious life in the Church and comes to the conclusion that satisfies him for the time being:

> Here is the clear and true meaning of *contemplata tradere* [to pass on what has been contemplated], expressed without equivocation by one who had lived that life to the full. It is the vocation to transforming union, to the height of the mystical life and of mystical experience, to the very transformation into Christ, that Christ living in us and directing all our actions might Himself draw men to desire and seek the same exalted union because of the joy and the sanctity and the supernatural vitality radiated by our example—or rather because of the secret influence of Christ living within us in complete possession of our souls.[11]

But Merton was growing. He never repudiated the basic insights of these early days—though he was later ashamed of some of the triumphalism. Rather, as he honestly searched and lived he honed them and saw their deeper human and divine implications. He was beginning to question. The cocky or defensive sureness that closes off all hope of growth was broken down in the real living of the life. In the closing pages

---

9. *Ibid.*

10. *Ibid.*, p. 414.

11. *Ibid.*, p. 418.

of the *The Seven Storey Mountain* he says: "By the time I made my vows, I decided that I was no longer sure what a contemplative was, or what the contemplative vocation was, or what my vocation was, and what our Cistercian vocation was."[12] He was ready to grow, and grow he did.

Twenty Years Later

Twenty years later we find not only a different Merton, but a different monastery, a different Church and a different world. If there was any true hope for a peaceful world in those years immediately after World War II, twenty years of constant wars of all sorts, accompanied with an equally constant arms buildup that was despoiling the earth, left little hope for a true peace in our times. The world, living under the shadow of nuclear annihilation, became a more desperate place, whether that desperation expressed itself in activism or escapism. The need for the monastic life was greater than ever, and this need was seen ever more clearly by Merton.

The Church, too, and the institutional monastic life of Gethsemani as a part of the Church, had been brought to a more realistic stance by the challenges of the Second Vatican Council. No room was left for complacency. Those who opened to the Council learned to live with questions and an ever expanding and deepening vision. Those who did not lived in an ever more threatened past. Merton was remarkably in touch with all of this and sensitive to it. He certainly had opened totally to the Spirit of the Council, and with a surer personal identity he faced and helped formulate the questions and challenges which he embraced with a joyful freedom. A few months before his death Merton prepared for the review of the Order a brief note on the "Renewal in Monastic Education," which

---

12. *Ibid.*, pp. 420-21.

was fated to be published in the same volume which would announce his untimely death and pay tribute to him.[13] In it we get a sense of the plenitude to which his monastic vision had grown:

> The monastic life is not only *contemplative* but *prophetic*. That is to say, it not only bears witness to a contemplative mystique of silence, enclosure and renunciation of active works, but it is alive in the eschatological mystery of the kingdom already shared and realized in the lives of those who have heard the word of God and have surrendered unconditionally to its demands in a vocation that (even when communal) has a distinctly "desert" quality.
>
> It should never be forgotten that the monastic life is a special way of living the gospel and that the monk's dedication to God by his vows (especially the vow to convert and transform his whole life in response to the word of God) is to be understood in the light of God's promises, the eschatological kingdom, and the recapitulation of all things in Christ.[14]

We find here a strong affirmation of his early evaluation of the monastic contemplative life and a stretching to something further and more transcendent in the proclamation of the eschatological character of the monastic way, a special way of living the gospels. But he goes on in the article to look not only to the transcendent future of monasticism but to its future on earth, and here we hear another new note:

> We need to form monks of the twentieth century who are capable of embracing in their contemplative aware-

---

13. "Renewal in Monastic Education" in *Cistercian Studies*, 3 (1968): 247-52.
14. *Ibid.*, pp. 248-49.

ness not only the theological dimensions of the mystery of Christ but also the possibilities of new understanding offered by non-Christian traditions and by the modern world of science and revolution.[15]

Here, Merton sums up in a nutshell the new influences that expanded his monastic consciousness: non-Christian religions, science and revolution. When speaking of "revolution" here, I don't assume that Merton was thinking exclusively or even primarily of bloody revolution, but more of the whole revolution in society, the culture revolution that has so radically altered the context of life for us all.

In his very last talk, Merton spoke of this new freedom, this transformation of consciousness:

> Christianity and Buddhism alike look primarily to a transformation of consciousness—a transformation and a liberation of the truth imprisoned in man by ignorance and error. . . .
>
> The traditional religions begin with the consciousness of the individual, seek to transform and liberate the truth in each person, with the idea that it will then communicate itself to others. Of course the man par excellence to whom this task is deputed is the monk.
>
> The monk is a man who has attained, or is about to attain, or seeks to attain, full realization. He dwells in the center of society as one who has attained realization—he knows the score. Not that he has acquired unusual or esoteric information, but he has come to experience the ground of his own being in such a way that he knows the secret of liberation and can somehow or other communicate this to others.[16]

---

15. *Ibid.*, p. 251.
16. *The Asian Journal of Thomas Merton*, p. 333.

Merton has relocated the monk. He is no longer on the outer margins of society, but at its center. And he has a task. He is not only to give witness to a contemplative mystique and the eschatological end of creation, but he is in some way, here and now, to communicate to others the secret of liberation, the way to transformation of consciousness. This care, this concern for others is a necessary corollary of transformation. Merton goes on to say:

> In the process of this change the individual ego was seen to be illusory and dissolved itself, and in place of this self-centered ego came the Christian person, who was no longer just the individual but was Christ dwelling in each one. So in each one of us the Christian person is that which is fully open to all other persons, because ultimately all other persons are Christ.[17]

In stating all of this, Merton is not conscious of departing in any way from monastic tradition. In fact he situates himself fully in it, appealing to the twelfth-century Cistercian Fathers, especially his friend, Adam of Perseigne and to Saint Benedict himself:

> When you stop to think a little bit about St. Benedict's concept of *conversio morum*, the most mysterious of our vows, which is actually the most essential, I believe it can be interpreted as a commitment to total inner trans- formation of one sort or another—a commitment to become a completely new man. It seems to me that that could be regarded as the end of the monastic life, and that no matter where one attempts to do this, that re- mains the essential thing.[18]

17. *Ibid.*, p. 334.
18. *Ibid.*, p. 337.

Having just evoked the Rule, he yet dares to plunge even deeper into his monastic tradition:

> What is essential in the monastic life is not embedded in buildings, is not embedded in clothing, is not necessarily even in a rule. It is something along the line of something deeper than a rule. It is concerned with the business of total inner transformation. All other things serve that end. I am just saying, in other words, what Cassian said in the first lecture on *puritas cordis*, purity of heart, that every monastic observance tends toward that.[19]

And he goes on to say:

> If you once penetrate by detachment and purity of heart to the inner secret of the ground of your ordinary experience, you attain to a liberty that nobody can touch, that nobody can effect, that no political change of circumstances can do anything to. I admit this is a bit idealistic. . . . But I am saying that somewhere behind our monasticism . . . is the belief that this kind of freedom and transcendence is somehow attainable.
>
> I, as a monk—and, I think, you as monks—can agree that we believe this to be the deepest and most essential thing in our lives, and because we believe this, we have given ourselves to the kind of life we have adopted.[20]

These were virtually the last public words that Merton uttered. He said a few more sentences and that was it.[21]

---

19. *Ibid.*, p. 340.

20. *Ibid.*, pp. 342-43.

21. They are important enough sentences: "I believe that our renewal consists precisely in deepening this understanding and this grasp of that which is most real. And I believe by openness to Buddhism, to Hinduism, and to these great Asian traditions, we stand a wonderful chance of learning more about

Final Integration

Merton saw a certain idealism in speaking about the goal which he truly believed was the goal of monasticism and was at the heart of every true monk, because it was his experience that the institutionalization of monasticism in the Church deliberately militated against the realization of this goal, and rather limited the aspirations of its subjects. He spoke of this very frankly in a paper he published just a few weeks prior to this final talk. "Final Integration: Toward a 'Monastic Therapy' " again demonstrates how contact with the East, with the non-Christian, awakened Merton to deeper penetration into his own tradition.[22] In this profound paper it is the work of a Persian psychoanalyst, Dr. Reza Arasteh, that serves Merton, though his thought ranges widely through many traditions.[23] After describing final integration, Merton goes on appealing to his own Christian monastic tradition and says:

This kind of maturity is exactly what the monastic life should produce. The monastic ideal is precisely this sort of freedom in the spirit, this liberation from the limits of all that is merely partial or fragmentary in a given culture. Monasticism calls for a breadth and universality of vision that sees everything in the light of the One Truth, as St. Benedict beheld all creation embraced "in one ray of the sun." This too is suggested at the end of chapter seven of the Rule where St. Benedict speaks of the new identity, the new mode of being of the monk who no longer practices the various degrees of humility with concentrated and studied effort, but with dynamic

the potentiality of our own traditions, because they have gone, from the natural point of view, so much deeper into this than we have" (*ibid*).

22. "Final Integration: Toward a 'Monastic Therapy' " in *Monastic Studies*, 6 (1968): 87-99.

23. Reza Arasteh, *Final Integration in the Adult Personality*.

spontaneity "in the Spirit." It is suggested also in the "degrees of truth" and the "degrees of love" in St. Bernard's tracts on humility and on the love of God.[24]

"Seen from the viewpoint of monastic tradition," Merton adds, "the pattern of disintegration, existential moratorium and reintegration on a higher, universal level, is precisely what the monastic life is meant to provide."[25] And Merton turns to a bit of history himself. He notes that in the highly structured societies of medieval Europe, of India, of China and of Japan, the only place one could find the freedom for this kind of growth was as a monk, one who stepped out of the caste system and freed himself from society's social limitations. But today, it seems to be almost the opposite in our country and in our Church. The ever more ample freedom of the lay person does not always find an echo in the monasteries, where rather rule and guidelines and traditional expectations risk to tie down the individual. The restriction of communal service and obedience initially does liberate us from attachments and self-will, but by hanging on, by seeking to channel and control the energies of the Spirit "it frustrates and stifles growth beyond the median level. . . . It tolerates 'safe' moderate growth and blesses lack of growth. In fact it is in practice more tolerant of those who do *not* grow."[26]

Merton again appeals to the vows we take as disciples of Benedict: "The real aim of that monastic *conversatio* which we have not only mentally approved but actually vowed: We have dedicated ourselves to rebirth, to growth, to final maturity and integration."[27]

And then Merton states simply and clearly his understanding of the meaning of the call to monastic renewal:

24. "Final Integration: Toward a 'Monastic Therapy,' " pp. 94-95.
25. *Ibid.*, p. 96.
26. *Ibid.*
27. *Ibid.*

"Monastic renewal means a reshaping of structures so that they will not only permit such growth but favor and encourage it in everyone."[28]

Is Merton right? Is this where historical monasticism leads us, especially when we extend our horizons and look at all of monastic history, Christian and non-Christian, though even when we just look at our own tradition in depth, perhaps goaded on by the challenges of other traditions? I think there is something deep in every true monk and nun that will readily respond: Yes, our call is to transcendence and true freedom in the Spirit. Yes, our minds and hearts are made to embrace all the cosmos, to be one with Jesus in his universal redeeming mission, to lift all to the Father in a truly universal love. Merton never repudiated the basic practices of the monastic contemplative life, but he saw ever more clearly how they were meant to lead to a true transformation of consciousness. There is much more that could be said, much more that could be drawn from the writings of Thomas Merton with regard to the fruits of his transformation of consciousness: his full humanity, his universal compassion, his articulate social concern—this son of God as a true peacemaker. All of this, and necessarily so, is the fruit of transformation of consciousness, of having the "mind" which was in Christ Jesus.

---

28. *Ibid.*

A Huge Chorus of Living Beings
Synthetic Listening—Evolutionary Response

A huge chorus of living beings!

But, who is listening?

Thomas Merton was one who listened. As we page through the vast richness of his literary heritage, we can hear something of that huge chorus of living beings. Nature speaks through his early poetry with a gentleness and a charm that may have been lost somewhat in his later, more powerful poetic prose and anti-poetry,[1] but nature continued to speak out, especially in the joys of his journaling.[2] The volumes of his letters let us hear echoes of the voices of human persons, delightfully young and sapiently old, rich and poor in this world's goods and in the riches of the spirit, persons of high station and low, well known and hidden—they are all there in an array that amazes.[3] Especially do we hear through Merton the cries of the oppressed: Jews, blacks, native Americans, victims of war . . . and so many others.[4] He gives voice to activists, and to philosophers and poets without number. We hear the voice of the Church; he translated papal encyclicals and ecclesial documents and shared the resonances they awakened within his spirit. The Fathers of the Church and his own Cistercian Fathers, whom he loved so well, were deeply heard and allowed to speak again through him. Above all does he give voice to the silence of contemplation, the contempla-

---

1. See *The Collected Poems of Thomas Merton.*
2. See *A Vow of Conversation,* and *Thomas Merton in Alaska: Prelude to the Asian Journal,* as well as the other journals cited further on in these notes.
3. See the bibliography below for the available volumes of Merton's letters.
4. See for example, *The Nonviolent Alternative.*

tive experience of God, the Creator and Conductor of the huge
chorus of living created beings who deftly leads them into the
creation and exultation of a new world.[5]

Yes, Thomas Merton listened, with an exquisitely fine and
developed listening. He heard the voice of a new world, a
voice that spoke of promise and inspired hope. And he had an
exquisitely fine and developed ability to give that voice a new
voice in his writings.

Perhaps, though, the more valuable thing we can learn from
Merton is how we ourselves can become better listeners. The
listening that we are—and listening is something that we *are*,
rather than something we do or have—is something that has
been shaped by all those factors that have made us who we
are. We hear that huge chorus of witnesses only to the extent
that they fit into the listening that we are. Toward the end of
his life, Thomas Merton had evolved into an extraordinarily
open listener, who heard all in a synthesis that ultimately was
one voice, a voice that spoke of a new world, a world of unity
and harmony, a world that spoke of peace.

The Evolving Listener

It certainly was not always thus with Merton. Rather, it is
the fruit of a formative evolution. Let us take the example of
his listening for Catholicism. A deep prejudice had been bred
into him. It prevailed in the home of his maternal grandpar-
ents and in the anti-clerical France, in which he was born and
in which he later received part of his early education. It was
also present in the proper British world within which he
continued his education.[6] The proud young agnostic would

---

5. Merton always considered his *Seeds of Contemplation* or the later expanded
edition, *New Seeds of Contemplation*, as being one of his finest works.

6. See *The Seven Storey Mountain*, pp. 171-72; Mott, *The Seven Mountains of
Thomas Merton*, p. 63.

sweep away the simple faith of his French hosts, the Privats.[7] Yet, at the same time other influences played to soften the boundaries of his prejudice. His artist soul responded to the beautiful ruins that Catholicism left about him in France. His own father's appreciation of things Catholic, reflected in his sketchings, played its part.[8] So did the gentle kindness of the Privats and the quiet sureness of their faith. The poetry of Gerard Manley Hopkins made a deep mark in this man, who always saw himself more as a poet than a prose writer.[9] He was a philosopher, too, and the faithful Catholicism of a man of the stature of Etienne Gilson spoke deeply to him. Later he would write to Gilson: "To you and to Jacques Maritain, among others, I owe the Catholic faith."[10] Perhaps the quiet, caring presence of a devout Catholic, Elsie Hauck, in the family home did more than anything to dissolve the listening limits of the prejudice that was largely bred in that home, though the weight of the benign presence of Dan Walsh cannot be underestimated. Certainly the unexpected advice of Bramachari, a Hindu master, that he should study Augustine and Thomas à Kempis had a shattering effect on it.[11] Merton himself began to consciously press against the limitations of his prejudicial hearing until the moment of enlightenment when one of the huge chorus of living beings spoke to him. A poet, his beloved Hopkins, gave expression to his own deepest aspiration and opened the way to conversion.[12]

But Merton soon learned and came to realize more profoundly in the course of a dissipated summer that a transformation of his listening to reality in one area did not necessarily lead to a total transformation. In fact, it just gave his listening

---

7. *Ibid.*, p. 37.
8. See *The Seven Storey Mountain*, p. 83.
9. Mott, *The Seven Mountains*, pp. 63, 120, 123, 147, 179, 201.
10. *The School of Charity*, p. 31.
11. Mott, *The Seven Mountains*, p. 113.
12. *Ibid.*, p. 120.

a new direction in which it could nurture prejudices—prejudices which would embarrass an older, wiser and more open Merton.

It was not so much the confines of a cloistered life that narrowed Merton's listening. If anything, these confines awakened in him an ever wider listening. It was rather the confines of a narrowly conceived Catholic piety, almost the antithesis of a truly Catholic piety, that, even while it gave powerful impetus and direction to the young monk, built solid walls of prejudice around his mind.

Fortunately, there were wise spiritual fathers at Gethsemani. Dom Frederic Dunne appreciated well the zeal of this gifted young man, but knew the perniciousness of a wholesale rejection of one's past. He put Merton to work writing his autobiography, offering him a possibility to review the formative influences in his life and to make a more judicious discernment as to what needed to be rejected and what needed to be embraced albeit in a wholly new and renewing context. The undertaking was not wholly a success, but perhaps it was a very important step in the right direction. Dom Frederic's successor invited Merton to find the insight that would enable him to make the needed discernment when he set the still relatively young monk to the task of teaching his fellows something of the wisdom of the Greek Fathers. Here Merton discovered that there is some middle ground between the *bios praktikos*, life taken up with the things of this world and ascetical practices, and *theologia*, the pure contemplation which the zealous and idealistic young monk so eagerly sought. There is *theoria physike*, the perception and contemplative enjoyment of God within creation, the little *logoi*, the little "words" of God, the shadows and images of the Word of God within creation.[13]

There can be, as we all know, a giant step, indeed an almost

13. See chapter above "Thomas Merton and Byzantine Spirituality."

infinite gap, between the intellectual knowledge of something and that effective experiential knowledge that truly transforms our response to reality, that reshapes our existential listening. For Merton, that transforming moment came only quite some time after his study of the Greek Fathers.

A Transforming Moment

Students of Merton are sometimes surprised when they discover that this man, who published not only an autobiography but also a whole series of journals or quasi-journals, was in fact a very private person. The autobiography and the journals were carefully edited works, the fruit of rather selective editing. To some extent this was an editing required by the censors of his Order, but far more extensively it was an editing required by his own innate need for privacy.[14] Now that his letters are being published, we can get a far more candid picture of the man, for his letters tended to go straight from his heart through the typewriter to the recipient. The deeper the spiritual affinity Merton sensed with his correspondent, and it also seemed the farther away the correspondent was, the more open Merton tended to be. One of his most personal revelations about his own prayer life is found in a letter to Aziz Ch. Abdul, a Sufi who lived on the other side of the earth.[15] And it is in a correspondence that had to spend months passing through the underground, in a letter to Boris Pasternak, that we are let in on the very Jungian experience that effectively transformed Merton into a wide open listener, who clearly perceived the unifying principle within all.[16]

This same transforming experience he shared far less can-

---

14. See Mott, *The Seven Mountains,* p. 160.
15. *The Hidden Ground of Love,* pp. 63-64. Aziz lived in Karachi; he and Merton never met personally.
16. See chapter above "Growing into Compassion," pp. 27-29.

didly but with more explanation as to what it meant to him in *Conjectures of a Guilty Bystander:*

> In Louisville, at the corner of Fourth and Walnut, in the center of the shopping district, I was suddenly over-whelmed with the realization that I loved all those people, that they were mine and I theirs, that we could not be alien to one another even though we were total strangers. It was like awaking from a dream of separate-ness, of spurious self-isolation in a special world, the world of renunciation and supposed holiness. The whole illusion of a separate holy existence is a dream. . . .
>
> This sense of liberation from an illusory difference was such a relief and such a joy to me that I almost laughed out loud. And I suppose my happiness could have taken form in the words: "Thank God, thank God that I *am* like other men, that I am only a man among others." To think that for sixteen or seventeen years I have been taking seriously this pure illusion. . . .
>
> It is a glorious destiny to be a member of the human race. . . . Now I realize what we all are. And if only everybody could realize this! But it cannot be explained. There is no way of telling people that they are all walk-ing around shining like the sun. . . .
>
> My solitude, however, is not my own, for I see now how much it belongs to them—and that I have a respon-sibility for it in their regard, not just in my own. It is because I am one with them that I owe it to them to be alone, and when I am alone they are not "they" but my own self. There are no strangers!
>
> Then it was as if I suddenly saw the secret beauty of their hearts, the depths of their hearts where neither sin nor desire nor self-knowledge can reach, the core of their reality, the person that each one is in God's eyes.

If only they could all see themselves as they really *are*. If only we could see each other that way all the time. There would be no more war, no more hatred, no more cruelty, no more greed. . . . I suppose the big problem would be that we would fall down and worship each other. But this cannot be *seen*, only believed and "understood" by a peculiar gift. . . .

At the center of our being is a point of nothingness which is untouched by sin and by illusions, a point of pure truth, a point or spark which belongs entirely to God, which is never at our disposal, from which God disposes our lives, which is inaccessible to the fantasies of our own mind or the brutalities of our own will. This little point of nothingness and of *absolute poverty* is the pure glory of God in us. It is so to speak His name written in us, as our poverty, as our indigence, as our dependence, as our sonship. It is like a pure diamond, blazing with the invisible light of heaven. It is in everybody, and if we could see it we would see these billions of points of light coming together in the face and blaze of a sun that would make all the darkness and cruelty of life vanish completely. . . . I have no program for this seeing. It is only given. But the gate of heaven is everywhere.[17]

A Theological Exploration

I might theologize a bit more on this experience of Merton, using the scholastic theology that contributed much to his formation at one time in his life but which we might say he transcended or at least left behind as the chosen mode for the transmission of his own developing insights.

---

17. *Conjectures of a Guilty Bystander,* pp. 140ff.

Theology tells us, grounded of course on scriptural revelation and patristic development, that at baptism we are ontologically transformed, made partakers of the divine nature and life. At the same time the Spirit of God was given to us to be our Spirit, to dwell within us and to teach us all things, calling to mind all Jesus had taught. In order that the Spirit might function within us divinized humans in a way consonant with our participated divine nature, we were given a new set of faculties called the gifts of the Holy Spirit—"gifts" because they were freely given at baptism or the moment of our coming into grace, and "of the Holy Spirit" because they are the faculties through which the Spirit will act in our lives. Significant among the gifts for us here are the ones called understanding and wisdom. Through the activity of the Holy Spirit in the gift of understanding we come to sense what "stands under" (the Latin name for this gift is *intellectus* = *inter* + *legere*, to read what is within), to sense the divine within each created being which in some way participates in God's own goodness, truth and being. The Latin word for wisdom is *sapientia*—*sapere*, to savor, to taste. The activity of the Holy Spirit in the gift of wisdom enables us to "taste and see how good the Lord is." It gives a real experiential sense of God's goodness in all.

We are all given the gifts of the Holy Spirit at baptism, but most of us leave these gifts wrapped up on the shelf. God who made us knows us as no one else and respects us as no one else. God knows that the greatest thing about us is our freedom, because therein lies the power to love. And God is love. God will never violate human freedom. If we want to always function at a purely human level, we are allowed to. It is only when we are willing to let go of our rational control of consciousness and open the space for the Spirit to act in us through the gifts that we can begin to know and sense things as God knows and experiences them. This freedom to let go of our rational control and open to the divine activity is developed in us through the practice of contemplative prayer.

Merton describes his own practice of contemplative prayer, as we have mentioned, in a letter to a Sufi, Aziz Ch. Abdul.[18] This openness in contemplative prayer, which provides the space for the divine activity in our lives and calls it forth, spills over from our prayer time to all the other waking hours and even to the time of sleep. Sometimes the activity of the Spirit through these gifts is more subtle, other times it is more pronounced or dramatic, as it was for Merton at the corner of Fourth and Walnut. Undoubtedly, the Spirit was already at work in Merton before that morning, as he daily sought to sit in silence and openness, letting go of all the parameters of his listening, so that the whole huge chorus of living beings and their Choral Director could be heard in their fullness. And the Spirit continued to work in him after this specially perceived moment of transformation when his listening came together in a conscious synthesis. More and more he perceived on a conscious level what he experienced on the deeper level of the gifts, that the goodness, the beauty and the truth of the divine is really present in every living being, in the whole of God's creation.[19]

Through a lifetime evolution his listening opened out until it no longer set any limits, and God and all that is of God could enter in and be experienced in its oneness in the divine. The experiences that brought Thomas Merton to this were many. Many of them were unique and will remain unique to his truly unique life-journey. Yet, essentially it was his practice of contemplation where he continually let go and allowed the divine the freedom to open him up ever more. The Spirit enlightened him in the true synthesis of all and in the harmony of that huge chorus of living beings. In the midst of it he lived out a vision of a new world, where all division has fallen away and the

---

18. See chapter above, "Thomas Merton and Centering Prayer," p. 115.

19. I think the next to last week of Merton's life marvelously exemplifies this kind of synthetic listening in his life. This experience is related in the chapter above, "The Legacy of Merton's Pilgrimage to India," pp. 173-76.

divine goodness is perceived and enjoyed as present in all and through all.

Select Bibliography

Note: Merton's works have now appeared in many editions with different pagination and even textual variations. The citations do not always correspond to these editions.

Works by Thomas Merton

The Ascent to Truth (New York: Harcourt, Brace and Company, 1951).

The Asian Journal of Thomas Merton (New York: New Directions, 1973).

The Climate of Monastic Prayer, Cistercian Studies Series, vol. 1 (Spencer: Cistercian Publications, 1969).

The Collected Poems (New York: New Directions, 1977).

Conjectures of a Guilty Bystander (Garden City: Doubleday, 1966).

Contemplation in a World of Action (Garden City: Doubleday, 1971).

The Contemplative Life (Springfield: Templegate, 1976).

The Courage for Truth: The Letters of Thomas Merton to Writers, ed. Christine M. Bochen (San Diego: Harcourt, Brace and Company, 1994).

Disputed Questions (New York: Farrar, Straus and Giroux, 1960).

The Hidden Ground of Love: The Letters of Thomas Merton on Religious Experience and Social Concern, ed. William H. Shannon (New York: Farrar, Straus and Giroux, 1985).

"Honorable Reader": Reflections on My Work, ed. Robert E. Daggy (New York: Crossroad, 1989).

The Last of the Fathers: Saint Bernard of Clairvaux and the Encyclical Letter, Doctor Mellifluus (New York: Harcourt, Brace and Company, 1954).

Marthe, Marie, et Lazare (Bruges: Desclee de Brouwer, 1956).

Mystics and Zen Masters (New York: Farrar, Straus and Giroux, 1967).

The New Man (New York: Farrar, Straus and Giroux, 1961).

New Seeds of Contemplation (New York: New Directions, 1961).

No Man Is an Island (New York: Harcourt, Brace and Company, 1955).

Raids on the Unspeakable (New York: New Directions, 1966).

The Road to Joy: The Letters of Thomas Merton to New and Old Friends, ed. Robert E. Daggy (New York: Farrar, Straus and Giroux, 1989).

Run to the Mountains: The Journals of Thomas Merton, vol. 1, 1939-41 (San Francisco: Harper, 1995).

The School of Charity: The Letters of Thomas Merton on Religious Renewal and Spiritual Direction, ed. Patrick Hart (New York: Farrar, Straus and Giroux, 1990).

Seasons of Celebration (New York: Farrar, Straus and Giroux, 1965).

The Secular Journal of Thomas Merton (New York: Farrar, Straus and Cudahy, 1959).

Seeds of Destruction (New York: Farrar, Straus and Giroux, 1965).

Selected Poems of Thomas Merton (New York: New Directions, 1959).

The Seven Storey Mountain (New York: Harcourt, Brace and Company, 1948).

The Sign of Jonas (New York: Harcourt, Brace and Company, 1953).

The Spirit of Simplicity (Trappist: The Abbey of Gethsemani, 1948).

Spiritual Direction and Meditation (Collegeville: The Liturgical Press, 1960).

The Springs of Contemplation (New York: Farrar, Straus and Giroux, 1992).

Thirty Poems (New York: New Directions, 1944).

Thomas Merton in Alaska: Prelude to the Asian Journal. The Alaskan Conferences, Journals and Letters, ed. Robert E. Daggy (New York: New Directions, 1989).

A Thomas Merton Reader, ed. Thomas McDonnell (New York: Harcourt, Brace and World, 1962).

Thomas Merton on Saint Bernard, Cistercian Studies Series, vol. 9 (Kalamazoo: Cistercian Publications, 1980).

A Vow of Conversation: Journals 1964-1965, ed. Naomi Burton Stone (New York: Farrar, Straus and Giroux, 1988).

What Ought I To Do? Sayings of the Desert Fathers (Lexington: Stamperia del Santuccio, 1959).

The Wisdom of the Desert (London: Sheldon Press, 1960).

Witness to Freedom: The Letters of Thomas Merton in Times of Crisis, ed. William H. Shannon (New York: Farrar, Straus and Giroux, 1994).

Woods, Shore, Desert: A Notebook, May 1968 (Santa Fe: Museum of New Mexico Press, 1982).

Zen and the Birds of Appetite (New York: New Directions, 1968).

Boris Pasternak/Thomas Merton, *Six Letters* (Lexington: The King Library Press, 1973).

Thomas Merton/Rosemary Ruether, *At Home in the World* (Maryknoll: Orbis Books, 1995).

Works on Thomas Merton

Cooper, David. *Thomas Merton: The Art of Denial* (Athens: University of Georgia Press, 1989).

Cunningham, Lawrence S., ed. *Thomas Merton: Spiritual Master* (New York: Paulist Press, 1992).

Del Prete, Thomas. *Thomas Merton and the Education of the White Person* (Birmingham: Religious Education Press, 1990).

Forest, Jim. *Finding Your Center: A Journey with Thomas Merton* (Alresford, England: Hunt and Thorpe, 1994).

_____. *Living with Wisdom: A Life of Thomas Merton* (Maryknoll: Orbis, 1991).

Griffin, John Howard. *Follow the Ecstasy: The Hermitage Years of Thomas Merton* (Maryknoll: Orbis, 1993).

Hart Patrick, ed. *The Legacy of Thomas Merton*, Cistercian Studies Series, vol. 92 (Kalamazoo: Cistercian Publications, 1986).

_____. *The Message of Thomas Merton*, Cistercian Studies Series, vol. 42 (Kalamazoo: Cistercian Publications, 1981).

_____. *Thomas Merton, Monk—A Monastic Tribute* (New York: Sheed and Ward, 1974).

Kilcourse, George. *Ace of Freedoms* (Notre Dame: Notre Dame University Press, 1993).

Mott, Michael. *The Seven Mountains of Thomas Merton* (Boston: Houghton Mifflin, 1984).

Seitz, Ron. *Thomas Merton: Song for Nobody* (Liguori: Triumph Books, 1993).

Shannon, William H. *Silent Lamp* (New York: Crossroad, 1992).

Other Works

Arasteh, Reza. *Final Integration in the Adult Personality* (Leiden: E.J. Brill, 1965).

Bolshakoff, Sergius. *Russian Mystics*, Cistercian Studies Series, vol. 26 (Kalamazoo: Cistercian Publications, 1977).

Gilson, Etienne. *The Mystical Theology of Saint Bernard* (New York: Sheed and Ward, 1955).

Hallier, Amedee. *The Monastic Theology of Aelred of Rievaulx*, tr. Columban Heaney, Cistercian Studies Series, vol. 2 (Spencer: Cistercian Publications, 1969).

O'Donovan, Daniel, transl. *The Works of Bernard of Clairvaux,* Cistercian Fathers Series, vol. 19 (Kalamazoo: Cistercian Publications, 1977).

Pennington, Basil M. *Call to the Center* (Hyde Park: New City Press, 1995).

_____. *Centered Living* (New York: Doubleday, 1986).

_____. *Centering Prayer* (New York: Doubleday Image Book, 1982).

_____. *Daily We Touch Him* (New York: Doubleday, 1976).

_____. *O Holy Mountain* (New York: Doubleday, 1978).

_____. [edited by] *One Yet Two: Monastic Tradition East and West,* Cistercian Studies Series, vol. 29 (Kalamazoo: Cistercian Publications, 1976).

Perigo, Grace, transl. *The Letters of Adam of Perseigne,* Cistercian Fathers Series, vol. 21 (Kalamazoo: Cistercian Publications, 1976).

Rose of Lima, transl. *The Christmas Sermons of Blessed Guerric of Igny* (Trappist: The Abbey of Our Lady of Gethsemani, 1959).

Saint Benedict, *RB 1980. The Rule of Saint Benedict,* ed. Timothy Fry, O.S.B. (Collegeville: The Liturgical Press, 1981).

Scott James, Bruno, transl. *The Letters of Saint Bernard of Clairvaux* (London: Burns and Oates, 1953).

_____. *St. Bernard of Clairvaux Seen through His Selected Letters* (Chicago: Henry Regnery Company, 1953).

Zahn, Gordon C., ed. *The Nonviolent Alternative* (New York: Farrar, Straus and Giroux, 1980).

Audio Cassettes

Egan, Keith. *Solitude and Community: The Paradox of Life and Prayer* (Kansas City: NCR Cassettes, 1981).

Pennington, Basil M. *A Centered Life: A Practical Course on Centering Prayer* (Kansas City: NCR Cassettes, 1979).

Works of M. Basil Pennington on Thomas Merton

Books

Thomas Merton, Brother Monk: The Quest for True Freedom (San Francisco: Harper and Row, 1987).

A Retreat with Thomas Merton (Warwick: Amity House, 1988; Rockport: Element Books, 1991; New York: Continuum, 1994).

Rekolekcje Z Thomasem Mertonem, tr. A. Gomola (Poznam: Dom Wydawniczy Rebis, 1993).

[Edited with Introduction] *The Cistercian Spirit: A Symposium in Memory of Thomas Merton,* Cistercian Studies Series, vol. 3 (Spencer: Cistercian Publications, 1970).

[Edited with Introduction] *Toward an Integrated Humanity: Thomas Merton's Journey,* Cistercian Studies Series, vol. 103 (Kalamazoo: Cistercian Publications, 1988).

Articles

"Introduction" in *Getting It All Together: The Heritage of Thomas Merton,* ed. Timothy Mulhearn (Wilmington: Michael Glazier, 1984), pp. 13-18.

"Thomas Merton: An Experience of Spiritual Paternity in Our Time" in *Studies in Formative Spirituality,* 5 (1984): 229-44; *Tjurunga,* 26 (1984): 23-35.

"Thomas Merton. An Educator for our Times" unpublished (1984).

"Thomas Merton: A Historical Reality and Challenge" in *Word and Spirit,* 6 (1984): 123-37.

"The Legacy of Merton's Pilgrimage to India" in *In Spirit and Truth,* ed. Ignatius Viyagappa (Madras: Aikiya Alayam, 1985), pp. 185-93.

"Merton, Spiritual Guide for the 80s" in *Where We Are: American Catholics in the 1980's. A Celebration for Philip Scharper,* ed. Michael Glazier (Wilmington: Michael Glazier, 1985), pp. 179-91.

"The Merton Journals" unpublished (1985).

"Thomas Merton and Byzantine Spirituality" in *Diakonia*, 19 (1985): 105-17; *American Benedictine Review*, 38 (1987): 261-75.

Toward an Integrated Humanity: Thomas Merton's Journey, Cistercian Studies Series, vol. 103 (Kalamazoo: Cistercian Publications, 1988), pp. 132-48.

"The Circular Letters of Thomas Merton" in *Monastic Studies*, 16 (1986): 201-13.

"The Merton Collection at Boston College" in *The Merton Seasonal of Bellermine College*, 11 (1986): 8-10.

"A Merton Symposium at Kalamazoo" in *The Merton Seasonal of Bellermine College*, 11 (1986): 18-19.

"Thomas Merton and Centering Prayer" in *Review for Religious*, 45 (1986): 119-29; *Studies in Formative Spirituality*, 10 (1989): 37-48.

"Fourth and Walnut" in *The Mirror*, 23 (1988), no. 43, pp. 5-8.

"The Seven Freedoms: Thomas Merton's Quest for True Freedom" in *Theology Digest*, 35 (1988): 16-18.

"The Spiritual Father: Father Louis' Practice and Theory" in *Toward an Integrated Humanity: Thomas Merton's Journey*, Cistercian Studies Series, vol. 103 (Kalamazoo: Cistercian Publications, 1988), pp. 32-51.

"Thomas Merton and His Own Cistercian Tradition" in *Review for Religious*, 48 (1989): 38-47.

"Thomas Merton's Bell" in *Our Sunday Visitor*, 78 (1989), no. 35, p. 12.

"Thomas Merton's Bell Still Rings Out" in *The Mirror*, 25 (1989), no. 9, p. 16.

"Merton's Bell Rings Out in Thailand" in *The Merton Seasonal*, 15 (1990), no. 3, pp. 13-14.

"A Huge Chorus of Living Beings. Synthetic Listening—Evolutionary Response" unpublished (1990).

"Thomas Merton's Flight Toward Freedom?" in *Our Sunday Visitor*, 79 (1991), no. 32, p. 12.

"Like Father, Like Son: Bernard of Clairvaux and Thomas Merton" in *Bernardus Magister*, ed. John Sommerfeldt (Kalamazoo: Cistercian Publications, 1991), pp. 569-78.

"Father Louis' First Book: *The Spirit of Simplicity*" in *Studiosorum Speculum: Studies in Honor of Louis J. Lekai, O. Cist.*, ed. Francis Swietek and John R. Sommerfeldt (Kalamazoo: Cistercian Publications, 1993), pp. 305-20.

Book Reviews

Thomas Merton, *Contemplative Prayer* in *Theological Studies*, 31 (1970): 207-08.

Thomas Merton, *Woods, Shore, Desert. A Notebook. May, 1968* in *Cistercian Studies*, 19 (1984): [663]-[665].

Paul Wilkes, *Merton: A Film Biography* in *The Merton Seasonal of Bellermine College*, 9 (1984), no. 22, p. 4.

Michael Mott, *The Seven Mountains of Thomas Merton* in National Catholic Reporter, 21 (1985), no. 11, pp. 9-20.

Marquita Breit and Robert Daggy, *Thomas Merton. A Comprehensive Bibliography* in *The Merton Seasonal of Bellermine College*, 11 (1986), no. 3, pp. 18-19.

Anne E. Carr, *A Search for Wisdom and Spirit: Thomas Merton's Theology of the Self* in *Cithara*, 28 (1989), no. 2, pp. 71-72.

Also available from New City Press by M. Basil Pennington

CALL TO THE CENTER
The Gospel's Invitation to Deeper Prayer

Pennington demonstrates the spiritually enriching power of centering prayer when used in conjunction with scripture. *Call to the Center* contains thirty excerpts from Matthew's gospel with corresponding meditations that invite prayerful reflection through centering.

"Fr. Basil leads the reader in a very personal way to listen to the Word of God in the Gospel of Matthew. His meditations show us *how* to open ourselves to God who gives us love, peace and joy and *how* to share these gifts with others in our troubled world."

MORTON KELSEY
Author of The Other Side of Silence

ISBN 1-56548-070-8, **3d print.**
paperback, 5 3/8 x 8 1/2, 168 pp.